seasons in the wine country

seasons in the wine country

RECIPES FROM
THE CULINARY INSTITUTE OF AMERICA AT GREYSTONE

by CATE CONNIFF

photographs by ANNABELLE BREAKEY and FAITH ECHTERMEYER

CHRONICLE BOOKS
SAN FRANCISCO

THE CULINARY INSTITUTE OF AMERICA

PRESIDENT
Dr. Tim Ryan C.M.C. '77

VICE-PRESIDENT, CONTINUING EDUCATION
Mark Erickson C.M.C. '77

SENIOR DIRECTOR, CONTINUING EDUCATION
Sue Cussen

DIRECTOR OF INTELLECTUAL PROPERTY
Nathalie Fischer

EDITORIAL PROJECT MANAGER
Margaret Wheeler '00

EDITORIAL ASSISTANT
Shelly Malgee '08

Library of Congress Cataloging-in-Publication Data available.

ISBN 978-0-8118-6588-3

Manufactured in China.

Designed by Erik Boissonneault.
Prop styling by Carol Hacker.
Food styling by Karen Shinto.
Location photographs by Faith Echtermeyer.

10 9 8 7 6 5 4 3 2 1

Chronicle Books LLC
680 Second Street
San Francisco, California 94107

www.chroniclebooks.com

table of contents

acknowledgments

This is no doubt as close as I'll ever get to feeling a bit like the people who win an Academy Award and have thirty seconds to give a nod to all the people who made their accomplishment possible before the music starts. As I stumble through trying to thank even a fraction of the people who have brought this book to life in the space allotted me, I ask in advance forgiveness for any lapse I might make.

First off, I want to thank Maggie Wheeler, my editor at the CIA. Thanks for your patience, your professionalism, and your perennial good spirits. May anyone who wants to put a book together be so lucky. Thank you also to the CIA's president, Dr. Tim Ryan; vice president of continuing education, Mark Erickson; executive director of strategic initiatives, Greg Drescher; and Reuben Katz, all of whom with their leadership and vision made the seed of Greystone a successful reality.

The CIA has been my home since I moved to Napa Valley in 1994. I have had too many opportunities to be around chefs, farmers, artisan food producers, and people who grow grapes and make wine than any one person who loves to be around this clan of people should probably ever be given in a lifetime. Thank you all. You are the reason and inspiration for this book.

I always knew I wanted to do *Seasons in the Wine Country* with Chronicle Books. To Bill LeBlond, thanks for the faith and encouragement; and to Amy Treadwell and Sarah Billingsley, for the skillful guidance in getting this book where it needed to be; and to Vanessa Dina and Anne Donnard, for designing it. To photographers Faith Echtermeyer and Annabelle Breakey—and food stylist guru Karen Shinto—without you, all of this would only be words upon the page.

I get to go to work every day and learn something new from our faculty, the people who teach the students who walk through the doors at Greystone. I especially want to let Toni Sakaguchi, Bill Briwa, Lars Kronmark, Robert Jörin, Adam Busby, Almir DaFonseca, and Polly Lapettito know that you have made my time at Greystone full of more learning and eating and enjoyment than I can ever convey. To those who have built Greystone, day by day, project by project, the journey would not have been filled with laughter and purpose without you—Holly Briwa, Cyd DePreist, Jim DeJoy, Dianne Martinez, Christina Adamson, and everyone else who keeps things interesting and moving forward. To the memory of our collective friend, mentor, and Earth Mother, Catherine Brandel, without whom the reasons for starting Greystone would not have made sense to me.

And while sipping wine and mulling over its pairing with food seems, perhaps, the best job on Earth, I know that it takes a certain discipline of thought and eagerness to share that only rare people possess. To Traci Dutton, whose original voice and take on wine grace these pages, thank you for your persistence in the process.

To Hope Reinman, whose touch with all things sweet and baked brought my jumbled thoughts and ideas about many of the desserts into being with her talent and own sweet spirit— I would have been lost in coconut and peaches without you.

To all the writers I have met along the way and who have inspired me with their deft touch with words, especially Paula Disbrowe, a sidekick in crime and one of the best writers I know, *merci*. To Antonia Allegra, who has always encouraged me, thanks for your faith.

And since no one ever springs unformed, thanks to my family, especially my mother, Micky Angers Ayars, who drove all six of my siblings and me in a station wagon every summer from Chicago to Cape Cod, where we would tumble out onto the sand for fried clams at Lisa Jean's Clam Shack; and my sister, Chris Conniff O'Shea, who shared a love of date bars. And to my father, Dutch Conniff, thank you for all the conversations about cooking, among other things.

My life on the East Coast set the stage for everything I love about food and cooking. Thanks to Laura Faure, Liana Haubrich, Kass Hogan, and the memory of Paige McHugh, who taught me to be quiet in a garden, the peace of cooking in a kitchen, and much about the mystery that is me, and to Christian and Gooz Draz, and the memory of their mother, Zell Draz; they gave me a place in their hearts and their homes.

And most of all I give thanks to the grace of the two people and a dog who have made Napa Valley my home. Michael, my husband, who brought and kept me here with the life we have made (and trips to the coast for oysters); to Sara Marsten Bittner, who helped make living here home with all the walks and talks and friendship; and to Tazo, the Rhodesian ridgeback, whose noble spirit kept me company all along the way.

michael chiarello

In 1987, when as a twenty-four-year-old chef I moved to the Napa Valley, the first thing I realized was that each ingredient I purchased, each dish I prepared, and each wine I enjoyed was grown and crafted by the farmers, food producers, and winemakers who would become part of an extended family of my life in this unique spot on Earth.

When I opened Tra Vigne, the farmers' market was brought right to our back door. Neighbor and butcher friend Ernie Navone (and a gang of other Italians) would show up to tell a few stories and share what their expansive backyard gardens produced. All this in exchange for a bowl of pasta, a bite of rabbit, and an order for Ernie's great chicken-apple sausage. Joe and Ashley Crisione would show up with a flat of milky, ripe figs before lunch, only to have a plate of grilled house-cured pancetta-wrapped figs served with a drizzle of twenty-year-old balsamico in return. Don Watson (lamb and pig god of the valley) would then arrive to pick up our vegetable trimmings to feed his pigs, drop off a lamb that had been dry-aged for three weeks, and hold class for the young cooks on what makes lamb taste best. Just before lunch service, Barney Welsh of Forni-Brown-Welsh Gardens organic farm in Calistoga would arrive to give us a hug, plus thirty cases of organic handpicked greens, tomatoes, and herbs. And he was never without a box of samples we "had to taste": cavolo nero (rare then) and maybe some Grapoli tomatoes from seeds I had gathered on my last trip to Italy. Products like these made my food what it was. My job wasn't to cook them well, it was simply not to mess them up on the way to the table.

Over the years I was blessed with scores of Napa Valley friends who made and loved wine. Belle and Barney Rhodes, both Mondavi families, Jack and Jamie Davies, Milt and Barbara Eislee, the Trefethens, Larry Turley, Dan and Margaret Duckhorn, Kourner and Joan Rombauer, John Williams, Tony Soter, and many, many more. With them came Darrel Corti, Narsai David, and others famous in California for their exquisite taste. Through these friendships, I learned the stories of each vintner as expressed in every bottle that we shared.

These connections between food and wine and people has taught me the largest lesson in my life, one that I have made my culinary life's quest: the difference between taste and flavor. We experience taste in a number of ways through our senses— what food feels like in our mouths, what it smells like, looks, feels, and even sounds like. Flavor, for me, is more allusive.

As I braise a Don Watson lamb with some Forni-Brown-Welsh vegetables, serve it with some Crisione balsamic vinegar over dried figs, and open a bottle of Heitz Bella Oaks Cabernet, the stories of the people who brought these foods and wines to the world are in each bite and sip. Taste comes together with memory and friendship and conversation to create what I feel is flavor in all of its intricacies.

> "Get to know your favorite producers, share their stories at the table, surround that table with those you love, and you, too, will discover flavor like no other."

I encourage you to shop your farmers' markets and get to know your favorite producers, share their stories at the table, surround that table with those you love, and you, too, will discover flavor like no other. As you discover this flavor you will be supporting local organic farming, whose profits can be reinvested in sound practices and new products, keeping our food carbon footprint to a minimum. Seek out the best, simplest techniques that will enhance this flavor. Consume appropriate amounts (as you will be full sooner from your relationships with each ingredient). Relish the coming of each season—develop a hunger for the first asparagus, taste the smell of vine-ripe tomatoes, head to an orchard to pick your own heirloom apples, and settle in with a house filled with the warming aroma of long-braised dishes.

When The Culinary Institute of America was looking to create a second campus, the unique and fertile ground and the people who grew and raised and crafted food and wine on it made Napa Valley an ideal location. Now that the college has been open for more than fourteen years, tens of thousands of students who have spent time at Greystone have been touched in some way by the gospel of crafting flavorful food with a combination of culinary talent and the very best ingredients. These students have now gone on to spread this gospel, which in turn has probably influenced a meal near you. And the ripple effects go on to influence markets, butchers, and farmers everywhere to get on the local, seasonal, relationship-oriented bandwagon.

In Napa Valley, the cycles of the seasons are enhanced by the wine-grape farming cycles that frame each season.

Cover crops of mustard and fava beans "tell" you it's time to get these ingredients into the recipe lineup. Bud break says *asparagus*, *spring onions*, *green garlic*, and the *tiniest new potatoes*. *Verasion*, or the long, final stage of grapes' ripening, takes hold in late July, and you can be guaranteed that tomatoes are at their peak. Harvest finds picking crews working feverishly to beat the first rains. And when the rains start, when the vines go dormant, it's time to get out your braising pot for long-simmering meat dishes and tune up your hiking boots for the first mushroom foraging of the year.

You have an able guide to these seasons of the vineyard as expressed through food in Cate Conniff, who showed up at the door to Tra Vigne with a basket of fresh figs from a tree in her backyard as her calling card. I had a sense then that she had found a home here.

As an ongoing culinary student I have taken the knowledge passed on to me, cherished the techniques learned while a student at the CIA's Hyde Park campus, and shared this knowledge and these techniques with all who will listen. Whether I am cooking for my show on the Food Network, farming my family's organic grapes for Chiarello Vineyards, or working on a new menu for my Restaurant Bottega in Yountville, the flavor of my education shines through.

Embrace the season, breathe deep, and keep your footsteps on the planet soft.

Now, get cookin'.

introduction

Seeking to establish a West Coast presence, The Culinary Institute of America began a search in the 1980s for an inspired site to house what was to be the college's continuing education campus for people in the food, wine, and hospitality professions. More than fifty locations were visited, mostly in Northern California's wine country, but it was when then–CIA president Ferdinand Metz and current president Dr. Tim Ryan saw Greystone that they recognized immediately the potential the historic building—formerly Christian Brothers Winery—would have as a world-class teaching facility.

Considered the largest stone winery building in the world when it was completed in 1889, Greystone rises castle-like against Napa Valley's western hills, looking out onto the verdant vineyards that have brought American wine making into the spotlight. The rich agricultural area surrounding Greystone has inspired some of the nation's leading artisan bread bakers, cheese makers, farmers, and foragers—as well as wine-makers—providing, quite literally, the fertile soil of ingredients and talent in which to cultivate a new era of professional culinary and wine education.

There was a ferment of activity in Napa Valley in the late 1980s and early 1990s, a pulse of Northern California's wine country as mecca for food and wine in America. Wines from the area were on solid footing with the best that Europe had to offer, cultivated by a generation of winemakers driven by the pursuit of excellence. Drawn as a bee to blossoms, a new generation of talented chefs began to create a style of cooking uniquely crafted with the flavors of wine in mind. It was in this rich terrain of people, product, and place that the seeds of the world's premier culinary college took root in California.

The transformation of the majestic nineteenth-century building into one with a twenty-first-century purpose reflects the spirit of tradition and innovation that has infused CIA Greystone from the beginning. While honoring Greystone's architectural heritage, the CIA created a dynamic mix of old and new with the creation of a fifteen-thousand-square-foot open teaching kitchen, replete with fire truck–red cooking suites. The Wine Spectator Greystone Restaurant and Campus Store and Marketplace rounded out the campus when it opened its doors in August 1995.

From its genesis, CIA Greystone has promoted the thoughtful synthesis of food and wine, along with a revolutionary approach to bringing world cuisine to the American table.

From initial classes in Food and Wine Dynamics and Mastering Wine has sprung a comprehensive professional wine education program, housed in its own state-of-the-art Rudd Center for Professional Wine Studies. From a foundation course showcasing the traditional cooking of Asia, the Mediterranean, and Latin America has grown an entire family of renowned classes, conferences, and special programs under the Worlds of Flavor banner.

> "Drawn as a bee to blossoms, a new generation of talented chefs began to create a style of cooking uniquely crafted with the flavors of wine in mind."

CIA Greystone is all grown up now. The college's prestigious associate degree program had its Greystone launch in 2006, and more than sixty sections of its Baking and Pastry Arts Certificate Program have graduated from Greystone in the last fourteen years. Its annual Worlds of Flavor conference brings the most recognized experts on world cuisine to the campus for what has become, in just over a decade, the leading professional education event in the country on global cuisine. Public cooking demonstrations and culinary enthusiast classes offer new insights into the world of the professional chef, translated for the home cook. In a short time, the CIA's West Coast campus has become a hub of food and wine culture in America.

I am very lucky to have been able to be a part of this amazing ride from the beginning. I started working at Greystone nine months before it opened. Before then, I was a confirmed New Englander and was working with many of the East Coast's groundbreaking organic farmers, cheese makers, fishermen, and other food producers while employed by Bread & Circus Wholefoods Supermarkets out of Boston. But fate had other plans for me, and, as many of these sorts of stories begin, mine started with an affair of the heart when, while visiting Napa Valley for the first time, a man, now my husband, asked me to dinner.

As it happened, the restaurant we went to was Michael Chiarello's Tra Vigne. Two months later, while visiting the Napa Valley for the second time, I had something of a Garden of Eden story in reverse: I reached out to pick a perfectly plump and ripe fig from a one-hundred-year-old tree. I still remember that taste of my first fresh fig. And that of my first Dungeness crab at Thanksgiving, when sourdough bread and cold, unfiltered Chardonnay set a tradition we've carried on since that time. Two years, a wedding, and a move to Napa Valley later, I had the chance of a lifetime to start working for the CIA.

This place that I now call my home is a twenty-nine-mile stretch of some of the most breathtaking scenery in the world. Through the hard work of many, many visionaries, the land of the valley floor is an agricultural reserve, conserved for the growing of crops, now mostly grapes. But there are walnut trees and peach orchards, strawberry fields and grazing land for grass-fed beef, and small organic farms that grow greens and beans and all sorts of produce. And then there are the vineyards that surround us, the inspiration for the chapters of this book. They are a part of the rhythm of my days and the seasons passing by.

When you add the people who take all of these ingredients and work their culinary skill and magic and personality upon them, when you factor in the chefs and farmers and winemakers who live and work here, it is a perfect storm of people, place, and that which comes to us from fields, forests, the icy-cold nearby Pacific, and basking-in-the-sun grapes.

I hope that *Seasons in the Wine Country: Recipes from the Culinary Institute of America at Greystone* brings a bit of Napa Valley to your home kitchen. Check out a farmers' market, try a new wine, learn a cooking technique or two, and gather your own perfect storm of friends and food and times shared around a table.

—Cate Conniff

bud break

Spring comes early to the Napa Valley in a blaze of wild mustard glowing through vineyards and an effusive flowering of pink and white fruit trees—fragrant promises of the plums and peaches to come. Clouds wander periwinkle skies, and young lambs graze lush, deep green hillsides. The subtle seduction of warmth loosens the soil as the light of day lengthens. The exotic scent of citrus blossoms is in the air, along with birdsong and bee hum. Vineyards are tilled, fields are planted, translucent new growth pushes out toward the sun. It's about to begin, another bud break on the vines, another vintage of wine to be.

Many of spring's most ethereal foods—asparagus, peas, strawberries, tender greens—are fleeting and fragile, to be enjoyed as often as possible in this brief moment in time. Asparagus is at its most just-from-the-soil earthiness in Grilled Asparagus, Shaved Serrano Ham, and Fava Bean Salad with Sherry Vinaigrette (page 23) and shows its softer side in Asparagus Risotto with Goat Cheese, Dungeness Crab, and Meyer Lemon (page 35). Peas popped from the pod and just-picked mint awaken the senses to the new-life nature of the season in Spring Pea and Ricotta Gnocchi with Pancetta and Mint (page 33), and Lemon-Glazed Pound Cake with Rose Water Strawberries (page 54) evokes the sensual perfume of gardens as they begin to warm and loosen.

A light touch, a gentle coaxing of flavor, and bright colors from food—the moist influence of water in Steamed White Fish with Julienned Carrots and Spinach with Lemon–Green Onion Sauce (page 43), the delicacy of Crab Ravioli in Ginger Broth with Carrots and Fava Beans (page 39), and the scent of lavender opening in the sun infused into Lavender Crème Brûlée (page 51)—is all that is asked of the cook as windows open and stirring breezes start to pull us outside.

prosciutto, parmesan, and honey mustard palmiers

The almost hallucinatory sweep of yellow that is wild mustard through the vineyards harbingers the waning days of winter and the bursting forth of color in wine country in spring. And with this shift come flavors that awaken the senses, such as the sweet mustard used here.

Salty, tangy, and slightly sweet, these palmiers (the word refers to their palmlike shape), remind me of a wine-ready and zesty Mediterranean take on the 1960s hostess favorite, pigs in the proverbial blanket. Remarkably easy, they'll have even the novice cook looking like a pro.

MAKES 36 PIECES

1 sheet (6 to 8 ounces) prepared puff pastry, partially thawed

3 tablespoons sweet mustard

12 thin slices prosciutto (about 4 ounces)

¼ cup grated Parmesan cheese

1. Preheat the oven to 400°F.

2. If the puff pastry sheet is not already a 9-inch square, roll the dough to these dimensions on a lightly floured surface.

3. Brush the dough with the sweet mustard. Lay the prosciutto slices over the mustard in a single layer and sprinkle with the Parmesan cheese.

4. Place a piece of plastic wrap over the puff pastry and very lightly roll a rolling pin over the puff pastry to gently embed the ingredients into the pastry; this will help keep the ingredients from separating from the puff pastry.

5. Roll the two sides of the pastry in toward the center as tightly as possible until they meet. Wrap the roll tightly with plastic wrap and place in freezer until slightly frozen, about 20 minutes.

6. Line a baking sheet with parchment paper or a silicone liner. Unwrap the dough from the plastic wrap and slice into ¼-inch-thick slices. Arrange on the prepared baking sheets about 1 inch apart. Bake until golden brown, about 10 minutes. Serve warm.

Wine Pairing

For the perfect start to a spring meal, reach for a bottle of sparkling brut rosé. This slightly richer glass of bubbles can handle the salty, full flavors of these little bites.

chickpea-encrusted fried artichokes and sweet onions with soft-boiled egg tartar sauce

This recipe plays with many of spring's most subtle notes, including those of tarragon and young sweet onions, the flavors of slender new growth and freshly dug earth before the long, hot growing season begins.

This particular tartar sauce is a great alternative to those made with raw eggs—and so much better than a commercial tartar sauce. This makes about 1 cup and will keep in the refrigerator for up to 3 days.

From John Ash, executive chef at CIA Greystone's Sophisticated Palate program.

SERVES 4 TO 6

soft-boiled egg tartar sauce

2 large eggs

2 teaspoons Dijon mustard

1 teaspoon white wine vinegar, or as needed

⅔ cup mild olive or other vegetable oil, or as needed

2 tablespoons finely chopped sweet pickle

3 tablespoons finely chopped sweet onion, such as Vidalia, or green onion

2 tablespoons drained and chopped capers

2 teaspoons chopped fresh tarragon or dill

batter

1½ cups chickpea flour

3 tablespoons cornstarch

1½ teaspoons baking powder

¼ teaspoon garlic powder

½ teaspoon kosher salt

Pinch of cayenne pepper

1 cup warm water

artichokes and onions

Juice of 1 lemon

8 cups water

12 baby artichokes, 1 to 1½ inches each in diameter

3 tablespoons rice vinegar

1 tablespoon kosher or sea salt

2 to 4 cups vegetable oil, for frying

1 white onion (8 to 10 ounces), peeled and cut into ½-inch-thick slices

1 lemon, cut into eighths

1. For the sauce: Place the eggs in a small saucepan and add enough cold water to cover by 1 inch. Bring the water to a gentle boil over high heat. Remove the pan from the heat and let the eggs sit in the water for 4 minutes. Drain and rinse under cold water to cool the eggs.

2. Peel the eggs by cracking and peeling from the big end first. Break the eggs into a blender. Add the mustard and vinegar and pulse a couple of times. With the motor running, gradually add the oil until a smooth sauce is formed.

[recipe continues]

3. Place the mixture in a small bowl and gently stir in the pickle, onion, capers, and tarragon. Refrigerate, covered, for at least 30 minutes before serving.

4. For the batter: In a medium mixing bowl, stir the dry ingredients together. Whisk in the water until just blended. The batter will be very thick. Refrigerate for 30 minutes.

5. For the artichokes and onions: Pour the lemon juice into a medium bowl with 3 cups of the water.

6. Trim the baby artichokes by peeling off the outer leaves, leaving only the pale green to yellow leaves. Trim off the tops to remove all of the spines. With a paring knife, peel the stem down from the bottom and around the diameter of the heart to remove any tough outer fibers, and then trim off the very end of the stem. As each artichoke is trimmed, place it in the lemon water.

7. In a deep saucepan, bring the remaining 5 cups of water, the rice vinegar, and salt to a boil over medium-high heat. Drain the artichokes and add to the boiling water. Adjust the heat so that the liquid is simmering, place a plate on top of artichokes to hold them under the water, and simmer until the artichokes are easily pierced with a skewer or the point of a sharp paring knife, 8 to 10 minutes. Remove from the heat and let the artichokes cool to room temperature in the cooking liquid. Drain, cut the artichokes in half, remove any spiny purple leaves in the center, and pat dry.

8. In a heavy pot, heat 2 inches of oil to 375°F. Add the artichokes and onion to the batter and gently stir to coat. Using a large slotted spoon, scoop up about 4 artichokes and some of the onion slices, place in the oil, and fry until golden brown, about 3 minutes. Drain on a plate lined with paper towels and repeat with the rest of the vegetables. Serve warm, with tartar sauce and lemon wedges.

Wine Pairing

A dry rosé made from Grenache or Mourvedre echoes the Provençal flavors of this dish.

steamed organic eggs with green garlic, asparagus, and spinach with pain de mie croutons

Here's an example of scouting the best of simple ingredients to create a dish greater than the sum of its parts. The freshest of organic eggs are the focal point on this up-tempo riff on eggs Florentine. I get mine from nearby Longmeadow Ranch, but you can seek a source near where you live. Pain de mie is an ideal bread choice, but a good-quality soft white bread can easily fit the bill. Do try and find green garlic, as its mild pungency works especially well with the spinach and asparagus.

This makes a great brunch offering, as most everything can be done in advance and refrigerated. When ready to cook, just crack the eggs into the ramekins and steam.

From Chef Christopher Kostow, executive chef at Meadowood.

SERVES 4

2 tablespoons olive oil

Two ¼-inch slices pain de mie or similar white bread, cut into ¼-inch cubes (about 2 cups)

3 tablespoons butter

4 teaspoons minced green garlic

8 stalks asparagus (about 8 ounces), trimmed and cut into ⅛-inch slices

8 cups very loosely packed baby spinach (about 4 ounces)

⅛ teaspoon kosher salt, or as needed

4 large eggs

Freshly ground black pepper, as needed

Sea salt, as needed

1. In a large sauté pan over medium heat, warm the olive oil and add the bread cubes. Stir to coat and sauté, stirring frequently, until the cubes are crispy and golden brown, about 5 minutes. Remove from the pan and place on a plate. Reserve until needed.

2. Return the sauté pan to the heat and add the butter. Melt over medium heat and, when the butter is frothy, add the green garlic. Sweat (see Chef's Note), stirring often, until the garlic is very fragrant and softened but not browned, 1 to 2 minutes.

3. Add the asparagus and half of the spinach, tossing to coat with the butter and garlic. Cover the pan and let the spinach wilt for 1 minute. Add the remaining spinach, toss to coat, cover, and let the spinach wilt for an additional minute. Uncover the pan and sauté the mixture, stirring often, until the spinach is completely wilted, 2 to 3 more minutes. Sprinkle with the salt, transfer to a plate, and chill in the refrigerator.

4. Bring a couple of inches of water to a boil in a wok or pan that measures 2 inches larger than a steamer basket. The water level should be below the bottom of the steamer basket.

5. When the asparagus mixture has chilled, divide it among four 6-ounce ramekins. Break an egg over the top of the mixture in each ramekin, being careful to keep the yolk in the center. Place the ramekins in the steamer basket. Reduce the heat to medium. The water should be at a gentle simmer. Carefully set the basket over the simmering water, cover, and cook until the whites are set but the yolks are still runny, about 10 minutes.

6. Carefully remove the ramekins from the steamer basket and sprinkle about ½ cup of the bread cubes over each egg. Top each ramekin with a few grinds of black pepper and a few grains of sea salt. Serve and let guests know to break the yolk and combine the ingredients.

Wine Pairing

Find a high-acid Sauvignon Blanc to give you everything you need for this dish—flavors and aromas of tender, green herbs, mandarin oranges, and crushed white pepper.

| Chef's Note |

sweating

Sweating is a technique by which ingredients such as garlic, shallots, and vegetables are cooked in a small amount of fat over relatively low heat. Sweating used to imply the use of parchment paper, but is most commonly understood now as cooking in a covered pan to soften ingredients, allowing them to cook in their own juices without caramelizing.

grilled asparagus, shaved serrano ham, and fava bean salad with sherry vinaigrette

Fava beans are one of those foods that have such a fleeting season that I cook them in many dishes while they are young, small, and sweet, and then say adieu until next spring. Preparing them is a bit of a labor of love. First they are plucked out of their pods and blanched, and then the deep green gems are popped from their outer skins. Like shelling fresh peas, this is best undertaken when there are a few moments to sit on a stoop or a deck and let the day, along with the skins, slip away.

Grilling tends to both tame asparagus, in regard to making it somewhat more wine-friendly, and to give it a touch of char, which combines with the woody accent of barrel-aged sherry vinegar and the soul of expertly cured meat that is the best of serrano ham.

Adapted for the home kitchen from the Wine Spectator Greystone Restaurant.

SERVES 4

2 pounds fresh fava beans in pod

2 tablespoons finely minced shallot

2 tablespoons sherry vinegar

1 teaspoon fresh lemon juice

1 teaspoon finely chopped fresh tarragon

¼ teaspoon kosher salt

Few grinds of freshly grated black pepper

6 tablespoons extra-virgin olive oil

20 stalks thin, young asparagus (about 1 pound), tough ends trimmed

4 thin slices serrano ham (about 2 ounces), trimmed of excess fat and cut into bite-sized pieces

2 ounces Pecorino Romano cheese, thinly shaved with a vegetable peeler

1. In a medium saucepan, bring at least 2 quarts of well-salted water to a boil.

2. Remove the fava beans from their pods (there should be about 1 cup of beans). Have a large bowl of ice water on hand. Place the fava beans in the boiling water and cook until just tender, 2 to 3 minutes. Drain and place in the ice water to stop the cooking and set the color. Drain and peel the tough outer skin from each bean, discarding the skin. Reserve the beans until needed.

3. Place the shallot, sherry vinegar, lemon juice, tarragon, salt, and pepper in a medium bowl. Stir and let the mixture sit at room temperature for 30 minutes. Whisk in 4 tablespoons of the olive oil. Reserve until needed.

4. Prepare coals or set a gas grill to medium high.

5. Brush the asparagus with the remaining 2 tablespoons of olive oil and grill, depending on thickness, 4 to 6 minutes, rolling the asparagus so that each side takes on some grilled color. Remove from the grill.

6. Place 5 to 6 asparagus stalks on each salad plate. Toss the fava beans with the vinaigrette and spoon a quarter of the mixture over each plate. Sprinkle with the serrano ham and shaved cheese. Serve immediately.

Wine Pairing

Sangiovese, Barbara, or even Tempranillo rosé would stand up to the strong flavors of the grill without overpowering the dish.

spring greens, beet, and pine nut salad with laura chenel goat cheese crostini and greystone gardens honey

With tender, young greens from Forni-Brown-Welsh Gardens down the road from Greystone, honey from nearby hives, and goat cheese made just over the mountain, this recipe has a certain *terroir*—flavors that reflect a particular coming together of sun and soil, a sense of place expressed through food and wine. Perhaps you can find some of these ingredients from a farm near you and play with flavors that tell a story of where you live.

SERVES 4

lemon thyme vinaigrette

¼ cup fresh lemon juice

2 teaspoons finely minced shallot

1 teaspoon honey

½ teaspoon salt, or as needed

Pinch of freshly ground black pepper, or as needed

¾ cup olive oil

½ teaspoon fresh thyme leaves

salad

1 beet (about 6 ounces), trimmed, peeled, and cut into very thin matchstick pieces

Eight 1-inch baguette slices

1 tablespoon olive oil

6 ounces young goat cheese, preferably Laura Chenel

2 teaspoons finely minced fresh chives

1 teaspoon wildflower or wild herb honey

8 ounces spring green mix (about 8 cups loosely packed)

4 teaspoons pine nuts

¼ cup mixed edible, organic flowers, optional

1. Preheat the oven to 350°F.

2. For the vinaigrette: Place the lemon juice and shallot in a medium mixing bowl and allow to sit for 10 minutes. Add the honey, salt, and pepper. Slowly add the olive oil, whisking to emulsify. Add the thyme, stir to combine, and adjust the seasoning as necessary.

3. For the salad: Toss the beet with 2 tablespoons of the vinaigrette and allow to marinate while making the rest of the salad or for at least 15 minutes.

4. Lightly brush the baguette slices with the olive oil. Place in the oven and toast until lightly golden and crisp, 3 to 5 minutes. Remove from the oven.

5. Whip the goat cheese and chives in a food processor until the cheese becomes fluffy, 1 to 2 minutes. Spread about 1 tablespoon of the goat cheese mixture onto each baguette slice. Drizzle each piece of bread with ⅛ teaspoon of honey.

6. Just before you are ready to serve, place the greens in a large mixing bowl. Starting with 2 tablespoons of the vinaigrette, toss to lightly coat, adding more vinaigrette as necessary. Place a quarter of the greens (about 2 cups) on each plate and sprinkle a quarter of the pine nuts and the reserved beet matchsticks on each salad. Nestle two baguette slices onto each plate. If desired, sprinkle 1 tablespoon of edible flowers over each salad and serve.

Wine Pairing

Perfect with Pinot Noir *vin gris*. Like the salad—crisp, clean, and flavorful.

parsley and mint artichokes with spring garlic and lemon aïoli

In this recipe, artichokes are lightly steamed in olive oil with mint and parsley before meeting the green garlic aioli in a spring-ingredient lovefest. You'll probably have leftover aïoli: serve with crisp spring vegetables. If you don't want to use a raw egg in making the aïoli, blend the garlic paste with 1 cup of mayonnaise and season with lemon juice.

SERVES 4

aïoli

1 tablespoon finely minced green garlic

1 teaspoon salt

1 egg, at room temperature

Juice from ½ lemon

½ cup plus 1 tablespoon olive oil, or as needed

½ cup canola oil

artichokes

4 large artichokes, ¾ to 1 pound each

½ lemon

1 cup finely chopped fresh flat-leaf parsley

¼ cup finely chopped fresh mint

½ teaspoon salt

5 tablespoons olive oil

1. For the aïoli: Using a fork or a mortar and pestle, mash the green garlic and salt together to make a paste. Place the paste in a food processor with the egg and lemon juice. Blend until smooth. Combine the olive oil with the canola oil. With the processor running, add just a few drops of the oil and blend until the mixture begins to thicken, then add the rest of the oil in a thin, steady stream until the mixture is thick. Cover and refrigerate for at least 1 hour before serving.

2. For the artichokes: Cut about 1 inch off the top of each artichoke—the interior thistle part of the artichoke should be showing. Rub the lemon half over the top of each artichoke to keep it from browning. Using a paring knife or vegetable peeler, peel away the tough outer layer of the stem and bottom of the artichoke, rubbing the lemon over their exposed surfaces. Use a spoon to scoop out the fibrous choke and scrape away any thistle fuzz. Squeeze the rest of the lemon half into the hollowed cavities.

3. In a medium bowl, mix together the parsley, mint, and salt. Drizzle 1 tablespoon of the olive oil over the herb mixture and stir to create a loose pastelike mixture.

4. Place a quarter of the mixture in the hollow of each artichoke, then place them upside down in a pot large enough to hold them securely. Pour the remaining 4 tablespoons of the olive oil into the pot and add enough water to bring the liquid to about one-third of the way up the artichokes. Place a piece of parchment paper on top of the pot and cover with a tight-fitting lid.

5. Bring the liquid to a boil over medium-high heat. Reduce the heat to a bubbling simmer between medium and medium-high heat and cook just until a sharp paring knife can easily pierce the stem, about 30 minutes. Do not overcook. Remove from the heat. Remove the cover and parchment and allow the artichokes to cool in the liquid for about 10 minutes.

6. Remove the artichokes from the cooking liquid and scrape away any herbs still clinging to the artichokes. Place each artichoke on a large plate. Place about 2 tablespoons of the aïoli in each of 4 small ramekins and place one on each plate.

Wine Pairing

Pinot Grigio, with its racy acidity and lemony flavor is a sure bet with this garlicky dish.

minted english pea soup

Peas and mint are a traditional spring duo, here brought together with the slight tartness and body of crème fraîche. Unless you or a friend grow your own peas or you can nab some as they come into the farmers' market, good brands of frozen organic peas are often the better choice, as the sugars in fresh peas turn very quickly to starch. This soup serves about 1 cup per portion and can easily be doubled. For the peas, you will need about 4 pounds in the shell, or two 10-ounce packages of frozen peas.

SERVES 4

2 tablespoons olive oil

½ onion (about 4 ounces), cut into ¼-inch dice

1 quart vegetable or chicken stock

1 teaspoon kosher salt, or as needed

⅛ **teaspoon** ground white pepper, or as needed

1 quart shelled peas, fresh or frozen

16 fresh mint leaves (8 coarsely chopped, 8 reserved for garnish)

2 tablespoons coarsely chopped fresh flat-leaf parsley

¼ **cup** crème fraîche

1 lemon, cut into 8 wedges

1. In a large, deep skillet or stock pot over medium heat, heat the olive oil. Add the onion and sweat it until translucent but not browned, about 5 minutes.

2. Add the stock, salt, and pepper, increase the heat to medium-high, and bring to a simmer. Simmer for 5 minutes.

3. Add the peas, chopped mint, and parsley to the stock and bring the liquid back to a simmer. Simmer until peas turn bright green and are tender, about 5 minutes.

4. Place a fine-mesh sieve over a medium bowl. With an immersion or in a stand blender, purée the soup until smooth. You may need to do this in batches (see Chef's Note). Pour the puréed soup into the sieve (you can batch this as well). With the back of a large spoon, push the liquid through the solids into the bowl.

5. Wipe clean the original pan. Pour the soup back into it and gently rewarm over medium-low heat. Add the crème fraîche and stir well to blend. Immediately remove from the heat, adjust seasonings as necessary, and pour the soup into small soup bowls. Garnish each bowl with 2 mint leaves and serve each bowl with 2 lemon wedges, for guests to squeeze into their soup as desired.

Wine Pairing

For an elegant match, try to find a lightly oaked or unoaked Chardonnay to complement the clean, fresh flavors.

| Chef's Note |

When puréeing hot liquids in a blender, be sure to remove the plug from the blender's top and cover the hole with a kitchen towel. This allows the steam from the hot liquid to escape.

simply cooked broccoli rabe

Broccoli rabe is another of the winter-to-spring bridge foods, as it is best during the cooler, softer days before the heat of summer. Blanching rabe (also known as rapini) takes off just enough of its bitter edge to make it a good partner with mustard-based dishes.

SERVES 4

1 pound broccoli rabe, thick stems cut off, leaves and sprouts coarsely chopped into 1-inch pieces and rinsed well

2 tablespoons extra-virgin olive oil

2 teaspoons minced garlic

Pinch of red pepper flakes

½ teaspoon salt

Freshly ground black pepper

2 tablespoons chicken stock, or as needed

1. Bring a large pot of well-salted water to a boil over high heat. Have a large bowl of ice water on hand (see page 41). Add the broccoli rabe to the water and blanch until just tender and still bright green, about 2 minutes. Drain and immediately place in the ice water to stop the cooking. Drain again and pat well.

2. Heat the olive oil in a large sauté pan over medium heat. Add the garlic and sauté until fragrant, about 1 minute. Add the broccoli rabe. Season with red pepper flakes, salt, and pepper. Add the chicken stock and sauté, stirring frequently, until tender, about 6 minutes. Serve immediately.

olive oil–potato coulis with green garlic and chives

Green garlic has a fleeting season, when the bulbs of the immature plant have yet to form and its mild garlic flavor pairs with other delicate flavors of spring. In this instance, its essence is gently infused into milk, where it releases a quieter effect than its much bolder summer evolution.

Try to find a young, fruity olive oil, new harvest if available, to finish the coulis, as it will be acting as a flavoring in lieu of butter.

SERVES 6

3 pounds Yukon gold potatoes, peeled and quartered

½ cup low-fat or whole milk, or heavy cream

2 tablespoons finely minced green garlic

2 tablespoons minced fresh chives

1 teaspoon kosher salt, or as needed

¼ teaspoon freshly ground black pepper, or as needed

¼ cup extra-virgin olive oil

1. In a large pot, cover the potatoes with cold water. Bring to a boil over high heat, then turn down to a simmer. Cook, uncovered, until the potatoes are tender, 25 to 30 minutes.

2. While the potatoes are cooking, place the milk and garlic in a small saucepan. Bring to a gentle simmer over low heat and cook until the garlic releases its aroma, about 4 minutes. Remove from the heat and allow the milk to steep with the green garlic for at least 20 minutes.

3. When the potatoes are tender, drain well and return to the empty pot. Cook over medium heat, shaking the pan frequently, until any excess moisture evaporates, about 3 minutes. Put the potatoes through a potato ricer into a large mixing bowl.

4. Drizzle the milk and green garlic mixture over the potatoes, sprinkle with chives, and season with salt and pepper. Stir gently to combine. Spoon the potatoes into 6 serving bowls and then drizzle about 2 teaspoons of olive oil over each serving. Serve immediately.

spring pea and ricotta gnocchi with pancetta and mint

One of the most fleeting of spring's foods in this part of the world is fresh sheep's milk ricotta from Bellwether Farms in Sonoma County. The sheep's milk is at its most sweet and grassy, and the cheese made from it is just a few days old. If you can find a fresh ricotta from a regional cheesemaker where you live, this would be the recipe to use it in. If not, buy the best whole-milk ricotta you can find. Ricotta gnocchi are traditionally from northern Italy. These have a ball shape and are lighter than their potato gnocchi cousins.

SERVES 6

¾ **cup** sheep's milk ricotta

2 **cups** shelled fresh peas, about 2 pounds 8 ounces in pod (about 10 cups frozen)

2 **cups** loosely packed fresh flat-leaf parsley leaves

1 **teaspoon** kosher salt, or as needed

¼ **teaspoon** finely grated nutmeg (see Chef's Note)

½ **teaspoon** freshly ground black pepper, or as needed

2 egg yolks

1 **cup** all-purpose flour

¾ **cup** finely grated Parmigiano-Reggiano cheese, plus more for garnish

6 **tablespoons** butter

3 **ounces** pancetta, finely diced

12 fresh mint leaves, torn into small pieces

1. Place the ricotta in a fine-mesh sieve over a bowl. Allow to drain in the refrigerator, covered, for at least 2 or up to 4 hours.

2. In a medium saucepan, bring 6 quarts of salted water to a rapid boil over high heat. Have a bowl of ice water on hand (see page 41). Add the peas and blanch until just tender, 3 to 5 minutes, depending on size. Add the parsley and cook 30 seconds more. Drain the peas and parsley and immediately place in the ice water to stop the cooking and cool completely.

3. Drain the peas and parsley well and transfer to a food processor. Process to a fine purée, about 30 seconds. Add the 1 teaspoon salt, nutmeg, ½ teaspoon pepper, ricotta, and egg yolks. Process until just combined, then transfer the mixture to a mixing bowl. Add the flour and the ¾ cup grated Parmigiano-Reggiano and mix thoroughly with a spoon.

4. Bring 6 quarts of water to a boil.

5. Using well-floured hands, roll the dough into balls about ¾ inch in diameter and lay the balls on a floured baking sheet.

[recipe continues]

6. Melt the butter in a skillet over medium heat. Add the pancetta and cook, stirring often, until the pancetta and butter are lightly browned, about 7 minutes. Remove from the heat.

7. Working in batches of no more than 10, cook the gnocchi in the boiling water until tender throughout, about 4 minutes. Remove them from the water with a slotted spoon and transfer to the skillet with the butter and pancetta. When all of the gnocchi are cooked, toss them gently in the skillet, season with salt and pepper, and transfer to a serving bowl. Garnish with torn mint leaves and Parmigiano-Reggiano.

Wine Pairing

Chef David Katz, who teaches Food and Wine Pairing classes at Greystone and is the proprietor of Panevino Catering, recommends a crisp Chardonnay with not much oak to accompany this dish.

| Chef's Note |

The difference that freshly ground nutmeg can make in keeping a dish fresh tasting is significant. Nutmeg graters are readily available and worth the small investment.

asparagus risotto with goat cheese, dungeness crab, and meyer lemon

This recipe, from Michael Pryor, previously sommelier at Greystone's restaurant and now winery chef at Langtry Estates Winery, plays with the flavor contrast between goat cheese that is just days old and goat cheese that is aged and more assertive. This bright risotto is also excellent without the crab.

SERVES 4 TO 6 AS A FIRST COURSE, 2 TO 3 AS A MAIN COURSE

---

1 bunch asparagus (about 1 pound), washed and ends trimmed off

¼ cup water

3 cups chicken stock

2 tablespoons butter

1 cup finely chopped onion

1 cup Arborio rice

¼ teaspoon kosher salt, or as needed

½ cup dry white wine

3 ounces fresh goat cheese, broken up into small pieces

3 tablespoons grated Parmesan cheese

6 ounces Dungeness crabmeat, picked over for shell

1 teaspoon minced lemon zest, preferably of a Meyer lemon

¼ teaspoon freshly ground black pepper, or as needed

2 tablespoons grated aged goat cheese

---

1. Bring a medium saucepan of water to a boil over high heat. Add a little salt to the boiling water. Have a large bowl of ice water on hand (see page 41). Add the asparagus and blanch until just cooked through and bright green, about 3 minutes. Remove and immediately place in the ice water to stop the cooking. Drain the asparagus and cut the stalks in half crosswise.

2. In a blender or food processor, blend the bottom halves of the asparagus with the ¼ cup water to make a thick purée, about 1 minute. Pass the purée through a fine-mesh sieve to remove the stringy parts. You should have about ¾ cup of purée. Reserve for the risotto. Cut the top halves of the asparagus into ½-inch-thick pieces and reserve in the refrigerator.

3. In a medium saucepan, warm the chicken stock over low heat.

4. In a heavy-bottomed medium saucepan, melt the butter over medium heat and add the onion. Sauté, stirring frequently, until just translucent, 4 to 5 minutes. Add the rice and sauté until it has turned slightly translucent, about 3 minutes. Add ¼ teaspoon of the salt and the wine and cook, stirring frequently, until almost all of the wine is absorbed, about 3 minutes.

5. Add ½ cup of warm chicken stock to the rice and cook, stirring very frequently, until the rice almost dries out, before adding another ½ cup of stock. Repeat until all of the stock is used.

6. Add the asparagus purée and continue to cook until almost absorbed, 2 to 3 minutes. Test the rice for doneness. The rice should be firm but cooked through. If it's not quite done, add a bit of water to continue cooking.

7. Add the fresh goat cheese, Parmesan, and the reserved asparagus pieces. Turn the heat to low and cook to heat the asparagus through, about 2 minutes. Add the crab and lemon zest and stir gently to heat through, being careful not to break up the crab. Adjust the seasoning with salt and pepper and serve with a sprinkle of grated goat cheese.

Wine Pairing

Delicious with a Sauvignon Blanc, in a Fumé style, that may have a little oak and some Semillon blended in. The cheeses and crab demand the touch of richness Fumé style produces.

napa valley pizza with caramelized onions, new potatoes, fresh goat cheese, and arugula

New potatoes and spring onions just dug from still-cool earth, arugula picked when it is mild before heat, and fresh, young goat cheese come together in a pizza that is at its most flavorful in spring.

Making pizzas at home can become a weekly ritual; they are a simple but tasty way of gathering what is most ripe and ready in the season to adorn a thin and crisp crust. The potatoes and onions can be cooked in advance. Have the other ingredients at hand, and welcome your guests into the kitchen to help arrange the toppings and enjoy the first pizza as it comes out of the oven while the second one bakes.

Thanks to Chef Robert Jorin, master of all things yeasted and team leader of CIA Greystone's Baking and Pastry Certificate program.

MAKES TWO 11-INCH PIZZAS

---

dough

6 tablespoons milk

6 tablespoons water

2½ teaspoons active dry yeast (1 package)

¼ teaspoon sugar

3 tablespoons plus 4 teaspoons olive oil

½ teaspoon salt

2 cups unbleached all-purpose flour, plus more as needed

potatoes

¼ cup olive oil

12 ounces new potatoes, either fingerlings or creamers, cut as thinly as possible

1 teaspoon kosher salt

6 tablespoons water or chicken stock

onions

¼ cup olive oil

4 small red onions (6 to 8 ounces each), peeled and cut into ⅛-inch–thick slices

½ teaspoon kosher salt

2 teaspoons finely minced garlic

1 teaspoon finely chopped fresh rosemary

1 teaspoon finely chopped fresh marjoram

3 cups loosely packed arugula

3 tablespoons olive oil

Cornmeal for dusting

4 ounces grated mozzarella cheese

8 ounces very young goat cheese, crumbled

---

1. For the dough: Combine the milk and water in a small saucepan and gently warm over low heat to about 100°F.

2. Place the liquid in a large mixing bowl along with the yeast and sugar and stir to dissolve the yeast. Add the 3 tablespoons olive oil and the salt and stir to combine. Gradually add the 2 cups flour, stirring to make a soft, pliable dough that is moist but not sticky.

3. Turn the dough onto a well-floured work surface. Knead the dough, adding just enough flour to keep the dough from sticking to the surface, until the dough is smooth and shiny, about 5 minutes. Divide the dough in half. Oil each of two medium mixing bowls with 2 teaspoons of the remaining olive oil. Place a dough ball into each bowl, rolling to coat with oil. Cover each bowl with a kitchen towel and place in a warm, draft-free area.

4. Let the dough rise until it has almost doubled in volume, 40 to 60 minutes. Prepare the pizza toppings while the dough is rising.

5. Preheat the oven to 475°F with a pizza stone inside.

6. For the potatoes: In a large skillet, warm the olive oil over medium heat. Add the potatoes and salt and cook, stirring often to prevent sticking, until the potatoes just begin to soften, about 4 minutes. Add the water, cover, and cook until most of the liquid is absorbed, continuing to stir from time to time to prevent sticking, about 5 minutes. Reserve until needed.

7. For the onions: In a large pot or deep skillet, warm the olive oil over medium heat. Add the onions and salt and cook, stirring frequently, until the onions begin to wilt, 4 to 5 minutes. Add the garlic and cook 2 more minutes, stirring frequently. Cover, turn the heat to medium-low and cook, stirring occasionally, until the onions are completely tender, about 20 minutes. Reserve until needed.

8. Mix together the rosemary and marjoram in a small bowl. Place the arugula in a medium mixing bowl and toss with 1 tablespoon of the olive oil. Reserve until needed.

9. Once the dough has risen, gently punch it down. Roll one half of the dough into an 11-inch circle.

10. Sprinkle 1 tablespoon of the cornmeal onto a pizza peel or 2 sheet pans and lay the rolled-out dough onto the peel, shaking the peel a little to make sure the dough is not sticking. Brush the dough with 1 tablespoon of the olive oil. Lay half of the cooked onions over the dough. Sprinkle half of the mozzarella over the onions, followed by half of the cooked potatoes and then half of the goat cheese over the potatoes. Repeat with the remaining dough, 1 tablespoon oil, and toppings.

11. Open the oven door and very carefully pull out the rack holding the pizza stone. Quickly transfer the pizzas from the peel to the stone. Bake until the cheese is melted and the crust is golden, 8 to 10 minutes. The goat cheese will soften and spread but not melt completely. Remove the pizzas from the oven with the peel, place on a cutting board, and sprinkle each with half of the fresh herbs and top each with half of the arugula. Cut and serve immediately.

Wine Pairing

A lightly styled red wine, Pinot Noir or even Cabernet Franc, would go well with the soft cheese and peppery greens.

crab ravioli in ginger broth with carrots and fava beans

These ravioli can be made in advance and frozen, and using a piping bag makes their filling a tidy affair. Lobster can be easily substituted for the crab, and cooked and diced shrimp can be combined with either crab or lobster. Edamame or peas can be substituted for the fava beans.

Adapted for the home kitchen from a recipe by Chef David Thater of Greystone's special events group, who makes fresh pasta when serving this to guests at Greystone.

SERVES 8 AS A FIRST COURSE

4 ounces scallops or shrimp

¾ teaspoon kosher salt

1 egg white

12 ounces fresh lump crabmeat
(Dungeness or peekytoe, if available)

2 tablespoons finely minced green onion

2 tablespoons finely chopped fresh cilantro

3 tablespoons finely minced fresh ginger

1 egg

1 tablespoon water

Forty-eight 3-inch round wonton wrappers
(one 12-ounce package)

5 cups Spring Vegetable Broth (page 40)
or light vegetable broth

2 baby carrots, shaved into thin slices using a vegetable peeler

¼ cup shelled and peeled fava beans

2 tablespoons finely minced fresh chives as garnish

1. In a food processor, purée the scallops, ¼ teaspoon of the salt, and the egg white until a mousselike paste forms, about 1 minute. Refrigerate if not using right away.

2. In a medium mixing bowl, place the crab, green onion, cilantro, and 1 tablespoon of the ginger. Gently fold in the scallop mousse. Place the mixture in a piping bag with a standard tip or in a bowl, and refrigerate if not using right away.

3. In a small bowl, whisk the egg and water to blend. Line a baking sheet with parchment paper and cover with a dry towel.

4. Open the package of wonton wrappers and peel off 6 wrappers. Cover the rest with a slightly damp kitchen towel. Place the 6 wrappers side by side. Brush 3 of the wrappers with the egg wash. Pipe (or spoon) a heaping tablespoon of the crab filling in the center of the egg-washed wrappers. One by one, lay an unfilled wrapper on top of a filled wonton wrapper. Close tightly, pressing from just around the filling out to the edges to release any trapped air. As they are completed, place the ravioli on the baking sheet and cover with the towel. If using right away, place the ravioli in the refrigerator while making the broth. (If freezing, place them in the freezer. Once they are frozen, take them off the baking pan, place in a covered container, and return to the freezer.) Continue with remaining wrappers to make 24 ravioli.

5. Pour the vegetable broth into a large saucepan. Add the remaining 2 tablespoons ginger, bring to a simmer over medium heat, and simmer for 15 minutes. Strain. You should end up with about 1 quart of ginger-flavored broth.

6. Bring a large pot of well-salted water to a boil. Add the carrots and fava beans and blanch until just softened and brightly colored, about 2 minutes. Remove with a slotted spoon and reserve. Bring the water back to a boil. Add the ravioli and cook until translucent, 4 to 5 minutes. Drain.

7. To serve, place 3 ravioli in each of 8 shallow soup bowls. Ladle about ½ cup of warm broth into each bowl. Garnish each bowl with a few carrot slices and fava beans. Sprinkle with chives and serve immediately.

Wine Pairing

Blanc de blancs sparkling wine, made from Chardonnay grapes, would pair well, adding another texture to this lively dish.

spring vegetable broth

This delicate vegetable broth has a sense of spring tonic: light, refreshing, nutritious and cleansing to the palate. Commercial vegetable stocks can be somewhat bitter and oddly orange, so making this broth is well worth the effort, especially because it will be the foundation for soups and many other dishes. You can easily double the recipe and then freeze what you don't use.

MAKES ABOUT 6 CUPS

---

2 tablespoons olive oil

1 medium onion (about 8 ounces), peeled and roughly diced

2 carrots (about 4 ounces), peeled and roughly diced

2 celery stalks (about 4 ounces), roughly diced

1 fennel bulb (about 12 ounces), trimmed, cored, and roughly diced

1 leek (about 6 ounces), white and light green parts only, cleaned and cut into ½-inch slices

2 sprigs fresh thyme

4 peppercorns

6 coriander seeds (optional)

6 fennel seeds (optional)

1 teaspoon salt, or as needed

2 quarts water

---

1. In a large soup or stockpot, warm the olive oil over medium heat. Add all of the ingredients except the water and cook, partially covered and stirring frequently, until the vegetables have softened but are not browned, about 10 minutes.

2. Add the water, increase the heat to high, and bring the broth to a simmer.

3. Reduce the heat so that the liquid is simmering slowly. Partially cover and continue to simmer until the broth has taken on a light color and sweet vegetable flavor, about 40 minutes.

4. Strain the broth and discard the vegetables. Allow the broth to cool to room temperature and then refrigerate or freeze.

steaming and blanching

steaming

As a cooking technique, steaming is relatively simple, forgiving, and clean. In multitiered steamers, several different foods can be cooked at the same time, and in covered steamers, food can stay warm while finishing touches are made to sauces or accompaniments.

Choose a pan that is between 1 and 2 inches larger than the bottom of the steamer basket, so that the bottom of the basket rests at least ¾ inch above the water.

Always bring the water underneath the steamer to a boil first; food should never be added to a steamer when the water is cold, because accurate cooking times reflect adding food once the water has come to a boil and steam has been created. Once the water has come to a boil, adjust the heat to maintain a gentle simmer. Make sure that the water does not completely evaporate during cooking. It's handy to have a teakettle of boiling water at the ready in case you need to refill the pan or wok.

Whole pieces of fish can be placed directly onto steamer trays or inserts.

When cooking smaller pieces of food, such as dumplings, it's helpful to line the bottom of the steamer with parchment paper, spinach, lettuce, or the leaves of napa cabbage.

Allow enough room between pieces of food for the steam to circulate completely around the food for even, rapid cooking. When lining the steamer baskets with leaves, leave 1 inch around the perimeter of the basket to allow steam to circulate.

Turn the heat off before removing steamed foods and always open the lid of the steamer away from you. Using a pair of elbow-length cooking mitts is a good way to prevent burns.

---

blanching

Blanching is great for taking the raw edge off of vegetables before they are mixed with other ingredients. Blanching also loosens the tough skins of vegetables, such as fava beans, making the skins easy to peel off.

The basic blanching drill:
Bring a *large* amount of water to a boil—you don't want the temperature of the water to drop too much when you add the vegetables. If blanching to brighten colors and use the vegetables later, add a generous amount of salt to the boiling water.

Prepare an ice bath. Fill a bowl halfway with ice and add enough cold water to cover the ice.

If cooking a large amount of vegetables, do so in batches. Remove the vegetables from the boiling water with a slotted spoon and allow the water to come back to a boil in between batches. Typically, the vegetables cook for a very short amount of time, usually 30 seconds to 2 minutes.

Once the vegetables are removed, place in the ice-water bath to stop ("shock") the cooking process. This step should also take between 30 seconds and 2 minutes, depending on the quantity of vegetables and their thickness. If blanching in batches, try to replace the used ice bath with new, and much colder, water.

Drain well, pat dry, and, if not using right away, refrigerate.

steamed white fish with julienned carrots and spinach with lemon–green onion sauce

In Northern California, spring brings a brief and coveted local halibut catch of fish so moist and sweet that the mild effect of steam is all that a piece of this beautiful fish needs. Wherever you are, try to find halibut or another rich white fish that has not been previously frozen, if at all possible. You'll have extra sauce; serve over rice, other steamed vegetables, or even chicken breasts.

From chef-instructor Almir DaFonseca.

SERVES 4

---

lemon–green onion sauce

1 tablespoon plus ½ teaspoon kosher salt, or as needed

1 bunch green onions (about 2 ounces), roots and most of the dark green part trimmed away

2 tablespoons rice wine vinegar

1 tablespoon fresh lemon juice

1 tablespoon minced shallot

½ teaspoon sugar

Freshly ground black pepper, as needed

¾ cup canola oil

2 teaspoons toasted sesame oil

fish

1 teaspoon finely grated lemon zest

½ teaspoon salt

⅛ teaspoon freshly ground black pepper

2 ounces baby spinach leaves (about 1 quart loosely packed)

Four 6-ounce pieces of halibut (sea bass can be substituted)

8 ounces carrots, trimmed, peeled and cut into thin matchstick pieces (about 2 cups)

---

1. For the sauce: Bring a medium saucepan of water to a boil over medium-high heat. Add 1 tablespoon of salt to the water. Add the green onions and blanch until they are bright green and just softened, about 1 minute. Drain immediately.

2. Place the blanched green onions, vinegar, lemon juice, shallot, sugar, and pepper in a blender and purée for 20 seconds. With the blender running, slowly pour the oils through the open hole in the blender top to emulsify, about 30 seconds. Taste and adjust the seasonings if necessary.

3. For the fish: Mix together the lemon zest, salt, and pepper in a small bowl. Bring a couple of inches of water to a simmer over medium-high heat in a wok or pan 2 inches larger than a steamer basket. The water level should be below the bottom of the steamer basket. Place one layer of the spinach leaves in the top of the basket and lay the fish on top of the spinach. Sprinkle about ¼ teaspoon of the lemon zest mixture over each piece of fish. Place the carrots in the bottom steamer basket and tuck the remaining spinach leaves around the carrots. Place the covered steamer basket over the simmering water and cook just until fish flakes easily, about 10 minutes.

4. Divide the carrots and spinach among 4 dinner plates. Place a piece of fish on top of the carrots and spinach and drizzle the fish and vegetables with 1 to 2 tablespoons of sauce. Serve immediately.

Wine Pairing

Find a high-acid Sauvignon Blanc to give you everything you need for this dish—flavors and aromas of green herbs, mandarin oranges, and crushed white pepper.

roasted rack of lamb with herb-and-mustard crust

A little lamb, a bit of mustard, and a whiff of mint come together in this easy-to-assemble-and-serve dish. Ask your butcher to "french" the racks. This will trim away any meat clinging to the rib bones, leaving them ready to be picked up and nibbled. Serve the lamb with Olive Oil–Potato Coulis with Green Garlic and Chives (page 31) and Simply Cooked Broccoli Rabe (page 30).

Thanks to chef-instructor Bill Briwa.

SERVES 4 TO 6

---

2 racks of lamb (about 1¼ pounds each), frenched

2 garlic cloves, peeled and crushed

1 **teaspoon** kosher salt

½ **teaspoon** freshly ground black pepper

4 **tablespoons** extra-virgin olive oil

3 **tablespoons** whole-grain mustard

1 **tablespoon** finely chopped fresh mint

2 **tablespoons** finely chopped fresh flat-leaf parsley

1 **tablespoon** finely chopped fresh rosemary

2 **teaspoons** finely chopped fresh thyme

½ **cup** coarse fresh bread crumbs

---

1. Preheat the oven to 425°F.

2. Rub each rack of lamb with one of the crushed garlic cloves, then discard the garlic. Season the lamb with salt and pepper.

3. In a large skillet over medium-high heat, heat 2 tablespoons of the olive oil. One at a time, brown the lamb racks well on all sides, about 8 minutes total. Reserve on a plate at room temperature.

4. In a small bowl, combine the mustard, mint, parsley, rosemary, and thyme with 1 tablespoon of the olive oil to create a paste. Rub the paste over the lamb.

5. On a plate, toss the bread crumbs with the remaining 1 tablespoon of olive oil. Roll the lamb racks in the bread crumbs to coat evenly. Place the lamb on a wire rack on a baking sheet and place in the oven.

6. Roast the lamb until an instant-read thermometer inserted into the thickest part of the meat registers 125°F for rare or 135°F for medium-rare, 15 to 20 minutes. Remove from the oven, cover with aluminum foil, and let meat rest for 5 minutes before serving.

7. Carve the lamb racks into individual or double chops, as desired, by cutting in between the bones, and serve.

Wine Pairing

Any bottle of Syrah, from simple to complex, would shine next to this meaty dish.

Lesson in Wine:
rosés

Like peas and asparagus, the appearance of rosés in the marketplace signals that spring is upon us. Because they require no aging or barrel fermentation, rosés are often the first wines released in the spring, just a few brief months from when their grapes were harvested and crushed. The combination of lip-smacking red wine flavors with the satisfying quench of white wine makes rosé an exceptional wine to bridge the cold, quiet days of winter with the warmer, lighter days to come.

how are rosés made?

Generally speaking, there are three ways to make a wine pink. Blending white and red wines is one of these, typically used only in the crafting of some sparkling wines. The second method, often referred to as *vin gris* ("gray wine" in French), uses red grapes of a certain ripeness that are grown with the singular intention of making rosé. The varieties usually used have less capacity for color. Just after the red fruit is pressed, the juice is removed from the skins and then processed almost exactly like a white wine. These rosés have the palest pink appearance, limpid even, as though a white wine had just gasped and begun to bring color to its cheeks. In California, *vin gris* is usually made with Pinot Noir and provides fans of that red with a sort of sneak preview of the vintage's character in watercolor.

Lastly, a popular practice, known as *saignée,* or bleeding, draws off juice after a time, several hours to a full day, from pressed red grapes, giving the juice more time to be infused with the red wine character of the grape's skins. In addition to other names, these rosés are called *rosado* (Spanish) and *rosato* (Italian). The best of *saignée* rosés are refreshing and bright, as with a white wine, but with several markers for red wines: red, blue, and black fruit; spice; herbal tones; and suggestions of red wine texture.

A special note on blush wines: Sometimes they can be a bit sweet and even a little fizzy, but (a) not always; (b) it's really okay if they are; and (c) they are still rosés. A category of rosés that are a bit sweet, "blush" wines rose to prominence in the early 1980s as white Zinfandel stormed the market.

styles of rosé

A key understanding to have for the enjoyment of any of the "pink" wines is that each wine is different depending on the varietal or varietals of grapes used to make it. Just as a Syrah tastes different from a Merlot, a "pink" wine made from Syrah will taste different from one made from Merlot. If a red wine has a garnet color, sour cherry flavors, and mild tannins, its pale-as-a-tea rose counterpart will be similar, perhaps with sweet cherry cider aromas and not a hint of astringency. On the other end of the spectrum, grapes used to make full-bodied red wines that are inky and indigo in color, taste of blueberries and mint, and finish with pleasant plush tannins will produce bright magenta-pink wines with intense berry flavors and possibly a hint of bitterness. For the same reasons that this is true for white and red wines, rosés from cooler climates, such as those from the Carneros and the Russian River wine regions, will have a crisp texture, be higher in acid, and lower in alcohol, while warmer-climate rosés, such as those from the Oakville and Rutherford appellations, will be slightly softer and creamier, full of fruit, and higher in alcohol.

rosés and food

Because rosés are made with so many different grape varieties, their possibilities for "pinks" are almost endless. Lighter, more innocent rosés bring out the floral fragrance of strawberries and lemon and the just-from-the-ocean brininess of ocean white fish, crab, and shrimp. Heartier, more sultry rosés made from grapes such as Cabernet Sauvignon or Zinfandel make agreeable partners with salty ingredients such as prosciutto and pancetta, dishes made with fruity olive oils, and some of the season's most stellar ingredients, such as green garlic and spring onions.

storing and serving

When drinking any type of rosé, the rules are easy: Try to enjoy within a couple of years of the vintage, drink chilled from a lovely glass, and always have an extra bottle on hand for those who can't believe how good it can be.

rhubarb and strawberry shortcakes with gingered crème fraîche

Nestled in a corner of Napa Valley's agricultural reserve is a strawberry field and its roadside stand. Every spring we all keep our eyes peeled for its hand-painted sign saying "Open" to let us know that berry season has begun. Often still warm from the sun, these sweet and fragrant gems are usually sold in flats; I usually eat a few berries before even making it home—they are irresistible. Try to find a farm stand near you when the strawberry bug bites, as they are highly perishable when perfectly ripe, so the best ones rarely make it to stores. The balance of juicy strawberries and rhubarb, their tart counterpart in spring desserts, together with the refreshing spice of ginger bits raises this recipe above the usual strawberry shortcake fray. Note: You need to start a day in advance of serving. The not-too-sweet and vanilla-scented shortcakes let the flavor of the fruit shine through, while providing a light and flaky bed upon which the fruit juices and whipped cream come home to rest.

Inspiration for this recipe came from pastry chef–instructor Stephen Durfee, who before becoming a faculty member at Greystone was the pastry chef at the French Laundry.

MAKES 8 ROUND SHORTCAKES

rhubarb

1 pound rhubarb, cut into ½-inch cubes (about 1 quart)

¾ to 1 cup sugar, depending upon desired sweetness

One 2-inch piece fresh ginger, peeled and halved (about 1½ ounces)

2 cardamom pods

vanilla shortcakes

2 cups all-purpose flour

¼ teaspoon kosher salt

1 tablespoon baking powder

1 tablespoon sugar

One 2-inch section of a vanilla bean

1 cup heavy cream, or as needed

3 tablespoons melted butter

whipped cream and crème fraîche with ginger chips

½ cup crème fraîche

1 cup heavy cream

2 teaspoons sugar

½ cup ginger chips (see Chef's Note, page 50) or candied ginger, finely minced

2 cups fresh strawberries, cut into ½-inch-thick slices

1. For the rhubarb: Toss the rhubarb, sugar, ginger, and cardamom pods in a glass container. Cover and refrigerate overnight. Turn the mixture once or twice to evenly distribute the sugar.

2. Place a fine-mesh sieve over a medium saucepan. Gently pour the rhubarb mixture through the sieve into the saucepan to collect the accumulated juices. Remove the sieve with the rhubarb and place over a bowl. Remove and discard the ginger and cardamom.

3. Bring the liquid and any undissolved sugar in the saucepan to a boil over medium-high heat and cook, stirring gently, until all of the sugar dissolves, about 3 minutes. Add the rhubarb to the saucepan and cook, stirring occasionally, until the rhubarb just begins to soften, 3 to 4 minutes. Remove the rhubarb mixture from the heat and reserve at room temperature. The rhubarb will continue to soften as it sits.

[recipe continues]

4. For the shortcakes: Preheat the oven to 425°F.

5. Sift the dry ingredients into a large mixing bowl. Slit the vanilla bean and, using a sharp paring knife, scrape the seeds into flour mixture and reserve the pod for another use. Stir the flour mixture to distribute the vanilla seeds.

6. Add 1 cup cream and mix into the flour with a large wooden spoon or silicone spatula. Add more cream as necessary until the dry ingredients become a firm ball of dough with no dry spots; it should not be sticky.

7. Turn the dough onto a lightly floured surface and knead about 20 times, until the dough becomes smooth but not shiny, and firm but pliable. Pat the dough into a 9-inch square.

8. Using a 3-inch round cookie cutter, cut 8 rounds of biscuit dough as close to one another as possible, rerolling the dough gently if neccessary.

9. Brush each shortcake on both sides with the melted butter to lightly coat, and place on an ungreased baking sheet. Place in the oven and bake until puffed and lightly golden, about 15 minutes.

10. Place the shortcakes on a wire rack and allow to cool completely.

11. For the whipped cream: Place the stainless-steel bowl and whip attachment for an electric mixer in the freezer 10 minutes before whipping the cream. Place the crème fraîche, cream, and sugar in the chilled bowl and whip on medium-high speed until soft peaks form, 2 to 3 minutes. Gently stir in the ginger chips. Reserve in the refrigerator until needed.

12. Place the saucepan with the rhubarb mixture back on the stove over medium-high heat. Add the strawberries and cook until the strawberries are just heated through but still firm, about 2 minutes. Tease the shortcakes apart with a fork. Divide the rhubarb and strawberry mixture among the shortcakes (about ½ cup per serving) and finish each shortcake with a small dollop of whipped cream.

Wine Pairing

These are exquisite with a late-harvest Muscat, which provides another layer of fruity aroma to this spring dessert classic.

| Chef's Note |

Ginger chips from Ginger People are a great staple to have on hand to help balance the sweetness in many a pastry.

lavender crème brûlée

On my first visit to Napa Valley, on a late spring day after an endless and dreary Boston winter, I sat outdoors on a patio surrounded by beginning-to-bloom lavender, its fragrance barely, but unmistakably, in the air. I'll forever remember that afternoon, with the sound of a fountain and the gentle warmth of the sun on my skin. I recall thinking that this was as close to Provençe as I could ever hope to find in this country.

When cooking with lavender, I like to keep its flavor and fragrance subtle, as though opening a window onto a patch of lavender that is off in the distance. Infusing lavender's essence into warm milk does just that for this surprisingly easy-to-make dessert, providing a wisp and a whisper of its appeal.

Note: You need to start this recipe either early in the day or a day in advance of serving.

SERVES 6

---

3 cups heavy cream

1 tablespoon dried lavender

8 egg yolks

Pinch of kosher salt

½ cup plus 6 tablespoons sugar

---

1. Preheat the oven to 300°F.

2. In a large, heavy-bottomed saucepan, bring the cream and the lavender to a simmer over medium heat. Watch the cream carefully; it curdles easily. Immediately remove from the heat and let the lavender infuse the milk for 15 minutes.

3. Bring a teakettle full of water to a boil. Place a fine-mesh sieve over a 4- to 8-cup measuring cup.

4. While the lavender is infusing, place the egg yolks, salt, and the ½ cup sugar in a large mixing bowl. Whisk until smooth, about 2 minutes. Add about a third of the infused cream to the egg mixture, whisking continuously. Add the remaining cream and stir to combine. Strain the mixture and discard the lavender.

5. Pour the custard into six 6-ounce ramekins and place in a deep baking pan. Pour enough boiling water into the pan to come halfway up the sides of the ramekins. Place the pan in the middle of the oven and cook until the edges of the custard are set and a spot in the center still jiggles when moved, about 35 minutes.

6. Cool the ramekins on a wire rack. Wrap tightly with plastic and refrigerate for at least 8 hours or up to 2 days.

7. An hour before serving, place an oven rack about 2 inches away from the broiler.

8. Evenly sprinkle 1 tablespoon of the remaining sugar onto each of the ramekins. Place the ramekins on a baking sheet and place under the broiler.

9. Broil the custards until they more or less evenly caramelized, 3 to 4 minutes. Remove the ramekins from the oven, place on wire racks, and cool for about 10 minutes. Place back in the refrigerator and allow to chill for 2 hours before serving.

Wine Pairing

The rose petal scent of a late-harvest Gewürztraminer is a lovely complement to this fragrant dessert.

model bakery coconut cake with passion fruit mousse

When looking for a great cup of coffee, something sweet to nibble on, and the gathering of locals, you'll want to find your way to the Model Bakery in St. Helena when in town. This adaptation of the bakery's famous coconut cake is for very special occasions, and although the recipe looks long, it can be made in steps. The coconut cream is the top layer in a can of coconut milk. Open the can without shaking it and spoon out the hardened cream on top; there should be close to ½ cup of this cream in a 14-ounce can of regular (not light) coconut milk. For the sponge cake, start at least a day in advance and cool the cake in the pans overnight. It is best to assemble the cake with the mousse after the mousse has cooled for about 30 minutes but before it begins to set up to the degree that it is not completely spreadable (about an hour). Assemble the cake with the mousse and let it sit in the refrigerator for at least 2 hours before making the whipped cream frosting and frosting the cake.

Thanks to Elizabeth Solano, of the Model Bakery, for sharing this recipe.

MAKES ONE 9-INCH CAKE; SERVES 8 TO 10

sponge cake

1½ **cups** cake flour

2 **teaspoons** baking powder

10 eggs

1½ **cups** sugar

1 **teaspoon** vanilla extract

½ **cup** milk

¼ **cup** butter

passion fruit mousse

¼ **cup** cool water

2½ **teaspoons** unflavored gelatin (1 small packet)

5 **tablespoons** butter

⅔ **cup** sugar

10 **ounces** frozen passion fruit purée (about ¾ cup)

8 egg yolks

2 **cups** heavy cream

whipped cream–coconut frosting

1 **cup** heavy cream

½ **cup** coconut cream

½ **teaspoon** coconut extract

2 **tablespoons** sugar

2 **cups** sweetened shredded coconut

1. Preheat the oven to 350°F.

2. For the sponge cake: Lightly oil three 9-inch cake pans. Place parchment paper circles in the bottom of each pan. Lightly oil the top of the parchment circles. Set aside.

3. Sift the cake flour with the baking powder twice into a large mixing bowl.

4. In the bowl of a stand mixer fitted with a whisk attachment, combine the eggs, sugar, and vanilla and beat on medium-high speed until the eggs have doubled in volume, lightened in color, and have the consistency of soft whipped cream, 3 to 4 minutes.

5. In a small saucepan over low heat, combine the milk and butter and warm until the butter melts.

6. Sift the flour mixture into the egg mixture in three additions, turning the mixer on and off in short bursts until the flour is just mixed in.

7. Remove the bowl from the mixer and pour in the warm milk mixture, using a spatula to fold the liquid into the batter from the bottom up.

8. Divide the batter among the three cake pans and place them in the oven. Bake until the surface of the cakes are spongy and light golden brown and a toothpick inserted into the cakes comes out clean, about 30 minutes.

9. Let the cakes cool completely in the pans, at least 2 hours or up to overnight. When ready to assemble the cake, run a knife around the edges of the pan and unmold the cakes. Remove the parchment paper circles.

10. For the mousse: Place the water in a small bowl and sprinkle the gelatin over the top. Gently mix the gelatin into the water to work out lumps and create a smooth mixture. Set aside.

11. Place the butter in a double boiler over medium to medium-low heat. As soon as the butter has melted, add the sugar and passion fruit purée and stir until the purée melts. Adjust the heat until the mixture reaches a low simmer, then add the egg yolks. Whisk the egg yolks continuously until the mixture has the consistency of lemon curd, about 5 minutes. Add the gelatin mixture to the bowl and continue to whisk until the gelatin dissolves and starts to thicken the mixture, and the whisk leaves a trail on the surface, about 2 minutes.

12. Remove the bowl from the heat and pass the mixture through a fine-mesh sieve, pushing the liquid through the solids. Cool the mixture to room temperature while whipping the cream.

13. Place the cream in the stainless-steel bowl of an electric mixer fitted with a whip attachment and whip to soft peaks. As soon as the passion fruit mixture has cooled to room temperature, fold in the whipped cream. Place in the refrigerator to cool for at least 30 minutes but no more than an hour.

14. Place one of the cakes on a flat plate. Spread one-third of the passion fruit mousse in an even layer on top. Place the second cake on top of the first. Spread another third of the mousse on top of the cake. Place the remaining cake on top of the second. Spread the last third of the mousse on top of the cake, leaving 1 inch around its edge without mousse. Place the cake in the refrigerator for at least 2 hours to set.

15. For the frosting: Place the heavy cream, coconut cream, and coconut extract in the bowl of an electric mixer fitted with the whip attachment. Starting on medium speed, whip just until the mixture starts to thicken, about 1 minute. Add the sugar and increase the speed to high. Whip until medium-firm peaks form, 2 to 3 more minutes. Do not overwhip. Fold in 1 cup of the coconut.

16. Spread the coconut frosting over the sides of the cake and the rim of the top of cake that does not have mousse on it. Pat the remaining coconut over the frosting. Cut into wedges to serve.

lemon-glazed pound cake with rose water strawberries

After bud break, as the canopy of grape leaves begins to fill in, roses that punctuate the end of rows of vines begin to bloom. Roses are traditional; in France, where conditions are often more moist during the growing season, they supposedly play a sentry role, alerting the vineyard manager to the possibility of mildew. Whether fact or fancy, roses add a colorful counterpoint to the green of the grapevine.

The fragrance of roses and strawberries come together for a floral and earthy counterpoint to the tart touch of lemon in the pound cake. Lovely for tea, a spring dessert, or a lazy morning breakfast.

MAKES ONE 9-BY-5-BY-3-INCH CAKE; SERVES 12

---

lemon pound cake

½ **cup** butter

1½ **cups** all-purpose flour

1 **teaspoon** baking powder

½ **teaspoon** salt

1 **cup** sugar

2 eggs, at room temperature

½ **cup** buttermilk, at room temperature

Zest of 2 lemons, finely grated

lemon glaze

Juice of 1 lemon

3 **tablespoons** confectioners' sugar

strawberries

2 **cups** strawberries, hulled and cut into ⅛-inch slices

2 **tablespoons** organic culinary rose water

2 **tablespoons** sugar

---

1. Preheat the oven to 325°F.

2. For the cake: Leave the butter out at room temperature until it is still cool, but indents from gentle finger pressure.

3. Measure the flour, baking powder, and salt into a large mixing bowl and whisk to combine.

4. Place the butter in the bowl of a stand mixer fitted with a paddle attachment. Beat on medium speed until the butter is free of the paddles and clinging to the side of the bowl, 1 to 2 minutes. Add the sugar and continue to beat for another minute. Scrape the bowl down and beat until the mixture looks fluffy and well blended, another 1 to 2 minutes. Add the eggs one at a time, on low speed, stopping to scrape the bowl down as necessary.

5. Add about a third of the flour mixture to the creamed butter and turn the mixer on and off for about 15 seconds, or until the flour is just barely blended with the butter. Add ¼ cup of the buttermilk, turning the mixer on again for about 15 seconds, or just until blended. Add another a third of the flour mixture, then the remaining ¼ cup of buttermilk, following the same procedure, mixing just until blended. Do not worry about the sides of the bowl. Add the remaining third of the flour, mix until almost blended, and then add the lemon zest. Using a wooden spoon or silicone spatula, scrape the paddle and sides of the bowl and incorporate the lemon zest into the batter.

6. Spray a 9-inch loaf pan with cooking spray. Pour the batter into the pan, place in the oven, and bake until the cake has deep golden edges, the center has risen, and the crust is glossy, with a few fissures, about 55 minutes. A cake pin inserted into the middle should have a few moist crumbs sticking to it.

7. For the glaze: While the cake is baking, mix together the lemon juice and confectioners' sugar in a small bowl.

8. For the strawberries: Place the strawberries, rose water, and sugar in a medium bowl, mix to combine, and place in refrigerator.

9. Once the cake is baked, place the pan on a wire rack and allow the cake to cool for 10 minutes. Loosen the edges by tapping the pan firmly on the counter, then remove the cake from the pan. Place the cake on the rack.

10. While the cake is cooling, brush the glaze over the top of the cake. Remove the strawberries from refrigerator and allow them to come to room temperature.

11. Cut the cake into ½-inch-thick slices and place each slice on a small dessert plate. Spoon some of the strawberries over each slice and serve.

ripening

Summer in wine country is a long arc of sun and heat during the day, with cooler, often fog-infused nights. Grapes and vegetables ripen and deepen in flavor and hue, spring's blossoms sweeten into fruit, and grazing animals drift on caramel-colored hillsides.

Rosemary- and thyme-scented days give way, with relief, to gentle evenings when the last lingering late-night light fades from the valley like a slow-moving river to the sea. Forays to farmers' markets, gatherings from the garden, and visits to the coast offer the just-picked produce and still briny seafood that inspire many a memorable meal.

Summer colors tumble kaleidoscope-like from fruit stands and produce displays: tomato, pepper, and watermelon reds; melon orange and blushing peach extravagance; jewel tones of berries; and purple and crimson plums. Verdant greens and corn and apricot yellows cast a stained-glass glow that says "Take me home; now's the time."

Starting with stellar ingredients and keeping it simple is the mantra of summer cooking everywhere. The cook's role is to bring a deft touch to transforming the ripe and ready-to-eat ingredients of summer into meals where the flavors of the food are the stars of the show. Delicately dressed and coarse-salt sprinkled, Watermelon and Watercress Salad with Ricotta Salata (page 67) is sweet and savory, cold and juicy. Fire and ice come together in the wood-smoked and crispy-cold Cedar-Roasted Salmon with Tomato-Endive Salad (page 89), Fish Tacos with Citrus-Cucumber Relish and Pico de Gallo (page 85), and Green Mango Salad with Grilled Beef (page 68). Blackberry Ketchup (page 60) and the New American Cheese Course (page 105) take fruits down to their more sultry, spicy side, while Eggplant Sandwiches with Tomato Jam (page 77) concentrate the summer sun as the pendulum begins to swing, almost imperceptibly, toward fall. A few basic techniques—balancing a vinaigrette to perfectly dress a salad, making not-too-sweet and true-to-their-fruit sorbets, and creating contrasting tastes and textures in grilled foods and their accompaniments—can be endlessly varied for a repertoire of summer cooking no matter where you live.

blackberry ketchup

In the summer, on my almost daily walk down a driveway by the vineyard near our house, Tazo the Rhodesian Ridgeback and I make a stop by the blackberry bushes to see if the berries have turned a deep dark color and softened just enough to make them perfectly ripe. I would imagine that many of us have a blackberry story, some summer memory of their juice and stain and being young. This is a great condiment to use as a sauce for grilled and roasted meats. It's delicious drizzled over cooked meat, or as contributor Mark Erickson has found, used as a glaze during the cooking process to prevent lean meats from drying out and becoming stringy.

Don't be afraid to make a good-sized batch while the blackberry bushes near you are laden, as it keeps for many months if covered tightly and refrigerated.

From Mark Erickson, CIA's vice-president of continuing education and a Certified Master Chef

MAKES 3 CUPS

1 pound fresh or unsweetened frozen blackberries

1 cup red wine vinegar

1 cup water

1½ cups packed brown sugar

½ teaspoon ground cloves

½ teaspoon ground ginger

1 teaspoon ground cinnamon

½ teaspoon cayenne pepper

½ teaspoon salt

1 tablespoon butter

1. In a medium saucepan over medium heat, combine the berries, vinegar, water, brown sugar, spices, and salt. When they begin to boil, reduce the heat to a simmer. Simmer, uncovered, until the juices in the pan appear to thicken slightly, about 30 minutes.

2. Remove the pan from the heat and allow to cool slightly. Purée in a stand or immersion blender until smooth. Strain the purée through a fine-mesh sieve into a small bowl to remove the seeds.

3. Whisk the butter into the sauce. Pour into glass jars and cool completely before covering and refrigerating.

agua frescas

Agua frescas, literally "fresh waters," are a piece of the Mexican culture and tradition that is part of the people and flavors of Napa Valley. Dramatically served in large barrel-shaped containers, agua frescas are often found in farmers' markets in the area, where favorite vendors fill thermoses for thirsty customers. When making your own, try and find organic ingredients, if at all possible, and try other variations on the theme, such as strawberries and basil and peaches and cucumbers. Serve these with the fish tacos on page 85.

From chef-instructor Bill Briwa

citrus and cucumber refresher

This water tastes best without any added sugar. Although subtle, the flavor is distinctive and much more refreshing than plain water, with the bright zing of citrus, the astringency of cucumber, and the fragrance of fresh herbs.

MAKES 1 GALLON

---

1 English cucumber (about 1 pound), cut into ¼-inch slices

2 lemons (about 4 ounces each), cut into ¼-inch slices

1 orange (about 8 ounces), cut into ¼-inch slices

20 fresh mint or lemon verbena leaves (about 1 small bunch)

4 to 6 cups still mineral water

---

1. In a clear glass gallon container half filled with ice cubes, combine the cucumber and citrus slices and muddle lightly to release the flavor. Be careful not to break or mash: Whole slices are an important component of the look of the finished refresher.

2. Bruise the herb leaves lightly, add to the container, and top the mixture with mineral water. Stir the ingredients together and refrigerate to chill the water and allow flavors to mingle, about 20 minutes. Serve cold.

[recipe continues]

melon agua fresca

MAKES 6 TO 8 CUPS

½ melon or watermelon (4 pounds), rind removed, seeded, and cut into 1-inch pieces (about 1 quart)

1 quart cold water

¼ cup sugar, or as needed, depending upon the sweetness of the fruit

1 tablespoon fresh lime juice

1. In a blender or food processor, combine the melon, water, sugar, and lime juice and purée until smooth, about 1 minute.

2. Strain the mixture through a fine-mesh sieve into a pitcher, pushing the liquid through the solids.

hibiscus flower cooler

MAKES ABOUT 2 QUARTS

2 quarts water

¾ cup dried hibiscus flowers

¼ to ½ cup sugar or honey, depending on desired sweetness

1. Bring the water to a boil in a large soup pot over high heat. Add the hibiscus flowers and return to a boil. Reduce the heat to a simmer. Simmer for 1 minute.

2. Add the sugar and stir to dissolve. Strain the tea through a fine-mesh sieve and refrigerate until cold. Serve over ice.

parmesan gelato, prosciutto di parma, and mizuna salad

Cold, salty, and savory, this dish is meant for a hot summer night. The mizuna salad adds some bite and tartness to gelato, acting to cut though a bit of its creaminess.

SERVES 6

gelato

1 cup heavy cream

¾ cup grated Parmesan cheese

mizuna salad

1 teaspoon finely minced shallot

1 teaspoon fresh lemon juice

1 tablespoon extra-virgin olive oil

⅛ teaspoon salt, or as needed

Freshly ground black pepper, as needed

2 cups loosely packed mizuna greens, washed and dried (arugula can be substituted)

12 thin, crisp 2- to 3-inch plain cocktail crackers

6 very thinly slices of Parma prosciutto (about 4 ounces)

1. For the gelato: In a double-boiler over barely simmering water, gently warm the cream and grated Parmesan, stirring continuously, until the cheese has melted and the texture is smooth.

2. Place the mixture in a fine-mesh sieve over a small bowl and gently squeeze the liquid through any remaining solids. Cover the bowl with plastic wrap (do not allow the plastic to touch the mixture), and place in the freezer until firm, at least 2 hours. Thirty minutes before serving, pull the gelato from the freezer and allow to soften slightly at room temperature.

3. For the salad: While the gelato is setting, prepare the salad. Place the shallot and lemon juice in a small bowl and allow to sit for 30 minutes. Whisk in the olive oil and season with salt and pepper. Place the mizuna in a medium bowl, pour the dressing over the greens, and toss to lightly coat.

4. Scoop out a small amount of gelato (about 2 tablespoons) with a 1-ounce ice cream scoop. The texture of the gelato should be somewhat granular and flaky. Spread a little of the gelato on a cracker and gently twist a strip of prosciutto over the gelato. Repeat with the remaining crackers.

5. Place 2 crackers on each of 6 appetizer plates and divide the mizuna salad among the plates (about ⅓ cup per serving). Serve immediately.

Wine Pairing

Serve with a flavorful, fruit-laden but lean and acidic red wine. A Napa Valley Sangiovese would fit the bill and give a nod to the Italian origins of the dish. Because of the warmth of the valley, the Sangioveses here have lots of ripe red fruit—cranberry, sour cherry, and red currant—with beautiful touches of dried leaves and mushrooms.

Technique:
salad days

Both simple and subtle, the composition of a salad is an art. Sweet, salty, bitter, and nutty flavors mingle with crisp and soft textures, creating a whole greater than the sum of its parts. A few basic techniques can carry you through the fresh and colorful salads of summer; pears, hazelnuts, and blue cheese in fall; citrus and bitter greens in the cold months; and tender peas, fava beans, and new potatoes in spring.

making vinaigrettes

Oils and vinegars are the building blocks of vinaigrette, and using traditionally produced artisan oils and vinegars makes a big difference in creating a vinaigrette that brings out the best in salad ingredients. Although the classical ratio of oil to vinegar is 3 to 1, you can play around with this, depending upon what sort of oil (olive, canola, walnut), the acid you are using (red wine, Champagne, balsamic vinegars, and a myriad of citrus juices), and the delicateness or pungency of the salad ingredients. A rule of thumb: Too much vinegar creates a tartness that closes the throat; too much oil produces an overly oily texture in the salad.

Many vinaigrettes use shallots or garlic as part of their base. Chefs often recommend "blooming" (or macerating) the minced shallot or garlic in the vinegar for about 30 minutes before adding the oil, as this softens its raw flavor.

Key to creating a smooth vinaigrette is the emulsification of the oil with the vinegar. Without getting too technical, emulsification is a process where the oil and vinegar wrap around each other, creating a blended liquid. Placing other vinaigrette ingredients in a bowl and slowly drizzling oil into the mixture while using a wire whisk to whip the oil into vinegar is the best way to emulsify a vinaigrette; ingredients such as mustard help the process.

preparing greens

Tear the leaves of greens apart by hand (knives can blacken greens), wash well, and dry completely, as greens must be thoroughly dry for dressings to adhere to them. Most salad greens benefit from being "crisped," or placed back in the refrigerator until cold. If storing the prepared greens for any amount of time, use the produce, or crisper,

section of your refrigerator. Try placing a slightly damp towel in the bottom of a storage container and leaving it slightly open.

dressing a salad

Less is more when it comes to dressing a salad. The trick is to lightly coat the ingredients with no more vinaigrette than necessary to create a slight glimmer of oil. A wooden bowl with sloping sides is a good place to start. Drizzle a small amount of the vinaigrette around the inner rim of the bowl and then gently toss the salad into vinaigrette. See how well coated the ingredients are before adding more vinaigrette.

 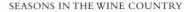

quinoa salad with basil and red bell pepper

Quinoa's nutty flavor and fluffy quality make for an appealing, light summer grain salad. The dressing here is a take on pesto, making it a good choice for tomatoes and other Mediterranean summer flavors and grilled foods. Blanching and shocking the basil creates a brilliant green color, and the omission of pine nuts makes it a lighter complement to the quinoa. The pine nuts are added instead as a salad component, where they lend a crunchy texture. You can substitute sunflower seeds for the pine nuts, and the salad would make a complete protein for vegetarians. The salad can be made in advance, refrigerated, and brought to room temperature before serving.

Thank you to Connie Guttersen, Ph.D., nutrition instructor at Greystone since 1995 and author of The Sonoma Diet *and* The Sonoma Diet Cookbook.

SERVES 8

⅔ **cup** quinoa

1⅓ **cups** cold water

¾ **teaspoon** kosher salt

2 **cups** lightly packed fresh basil leaves

2 **tablespoons** freshly grated Parmesan cheese

3 **tablespoons** fresh lemon juice

3 **tablespoons** extra-virgin olive oil

2 **teaspoons** minced garlic

1 red bell pepper, cored, seeded, and cut into ⅛-inch dice (about 6 ounces)

½ **cup** minced green onions

¼ **teaspoon** freshly ground black pepper

¼ **cup** pine nuts, lightly toasted

---

1. Place the quinoa in a small strainer and run under cold water. Drain.

2. In a small saucepan, combine the water, quinoa, and ¼ teaspoon salt. Stir and bring to a boil over high heat. Reduce the heat to a simmer over medium-low heat and cover. Simmer until the quinoa is tender, about 20 minutes. Fluff the quinoa with a fork and let stand to cool slightly, about 5 minutes. Drain off any of the remaining water and place in a large mixing bowl to completely cool.

3. In a small saucepan, bring 2 cups of water to a boil over high heat. Have a bowl of ice water on hand (see page 41). Add the basil leaves to the boiling water, stir once, and drain immediately. Place the basil in the ice bath to cool quickly. Drain and gently squeeze out any excess moisture.

4. Place the basil in the bowl of a food processor. Add the Parmesan cheese, lemon juice, olive oil, and garlic. Process until smooth, about 30 seconds.

5. Add the basil mixture to the quinoa, along with the red pepper and green onions. Stir gently to combine and season with the remaining ½ teaspoon salt and the pepper. Cover and refrigerate for up to 6 hours. Stir in the pine nuts just before serving.

Wine Pairing

A fresh, crisp white like Pinot Grigio will complement but not overpower the grain salad.

watermelon and watercress salad with ricotta salata

Executive sous-chef Josh Anderson likes ricotta salata's pure white color and mellow blend of nutty, milky, and salty flavors in this refreshing summer salad. You can substitute with feta cheese if you can't find ricotta salata. Fleur de sel becomes an important ingredient in a salad such as this, where its crunch and mineral taste act as counterpoints to the sweet juiciness of the watermelon.

Use the extra vinaigrette on corn on the cob, brush it on meats after they come off the grill, or toss it with cool, thinly sliced cucumbers straight from the refrigerator.

Adapted from the Wine Spectator Greystone Restaurant.

SERVES 6

golden balsamic sherry vinaigrette

1 shallot (about 1 ounce), minced

⅓ cup golden balsamic vinegar

2 tablespoons sherry vinegar

2 teaspoons chopped fresh thyme

1 cup fruity extra-virgin olive oil

½ teaspoon kosher salt

Freshly ground black pepper as needed

salad

6 thin slices serrano ham (about 4 ounces)

6 tablespoons pine nuts

1 bunch watercress or upland cress leaves (about 3 cups)

6 cups ½-inch cubes red and yellow seedless watermelon

5½ ounces ricotta salata cheese, cut into ¼-inch cubes

1 teaspoon fleur de sel

1. For the vinaigrette: Place the shallot, vinegars, and thyme in a small bowl and allow the shallot to "bloom" (macerate) for 30 minutes.

2. Drizzle in the olive oil, whisking to emulsify. Season with salt and pepper.

3. For the salad: Preheat the oven to 400°F. Place the serrano ham slices on a baking sheet, invert another baking sheet on top, and bake until crisp, 8 to 12 minutes. Remove from the baking sheet and cool.

4. Place the pine nuts in a small pan and toast over medium heat, shaking frequently, until just lightly golden brown, 4 to 5 minutes. Immediately pour the pine nuts onto a plate to cool.

5. Combine the watercress, watermelon, ricotta salata, and pine nuts in a large salad bowl.

6. Dress the salad starting with about ¼ cup of the vinaigrette and toss lightly to coat. Add more as needed, 1 tablespoon at a time.

7. Divide the salad onto 6 chilled salad plates. Sprinkle with fleur de sel and top each salad with a slice of serrano ham.

Wine Pairing

These flavors meld perfectly with a pale, dry rosé made from Cabernet Franc grapes, which echo the watermelon color and the peppery taste of the watercress.

green mango salad with grilled beef

In Vietnam the green mangoes commonly used in salads are a special variety grown to be eaten before they ripen. For this recipe, you can use any unripe mango, or you can substitute with Granny Smith apples. The smokiness of the beef juxtaposes nicely against the tart fruit. Flank or hanger steak can be substituted for the New York steak. For best flavor, try to leave a thin layer of the skin on the mango. It adds a wonderful texture and fragrance to the salad. Regular basil can be substituted for the Asian basil.

From Greg Drescher, executive director of Strategic Initiatives at the CIA, and his wife, Mai Pham, adjunct faculty member, chef-owner of Lemongrass Restaurant in Sacramento, and cookbook author.

SERVES 4 AS A GENEROUS FIRST COURSE OR LIGHT LUNCH

2 tablespoons minced lemongrass (see Chef's Note, page 70)

1½ teaspoons finely chopped shallot

2 teaspoons soy sauce

¼ cup sugar

8 ounces New York strip steak, 1 to 1½ inches thick, cut across the grain into ¼-inch-thick strips

1 green mango (about 1 pound), peeled, pitted, and cut into 3-inch-long thin strips, or 1 large Granny Smith apple (about 8 ounces), cored and cut into ⅛-inch-thick slices

¼ cup Chile-Lime Sauce (page 70)

1 tablespoon chopped fresh cilantro

¼ cup coarsely chopped fresh Asian basil leaves

2 tablespoons coarsely chopped roasted peanuts

2 tablespoons Fried Shallots (page 70)

1. Combine the lemongrass, shallot, soy sauce, and sugar in a bowl and stir well to combine. Add the beef, turning to coat, and marinate for 20 minutes.

2. Light a charcoal fire or turn a gas grill to medium-high. When the grill is ready (for a charcoal fire, you'll be able to hold your hand 5 inches above the coals for 3 to 4 seconds), drain the beef from the marinade and grill until the meat is just done, 2 to 3 minutes total (1 to 1½ minutes per side).

3. Place the mango in a mixing bowl and toss gently with enough chile-lime sauce to coat lightly. Add the beef, cilantro, basil, and peanuts. Toss gently, place on a small platter, sprinkle the fried shallots over the salad, and serve.

Wine Pairing

Mai sees the sweetness and smokiness of this dish as pairing well with a crisp, fruity Viognier or Riesling. Even with the beef, a bone-dry Riesling with bracingly high acidity is a great match for this dish, mimicking the green mango flavor.

chile-lime sauce

You'll have extra sauce, which can jazz up a simple cold noodle or rice salad.

MAKES ABOUT ½ CUP

---

2 small garlic cloves, peeled

3 Thai bird chiles (serrano or jalapeño chiles can be substituted)

3 tablespoons sugar

3 tablespoons fish sauce

3 tablespoons fresh lime juice, including some pulp

3 tablespoons water

---

1. Place the garlic, chiles, and sugar in a mortar and pound into a paste.

2. Transfer to a small mixing bowl and add the fish sauce, lime juice, and water. Stir to combine and let sit for 15 minutes so that the flavors can develop. The sauce will keep for up to 2 weeks, covered, in the refrigerator.

fried shallots

You'll need only a small portion of these shallots for this recipe, but they can be stored for up to 2 weeks in a tightly covered container in the refrigerator. They are great over other salads as a crisp counterpoint and with cold noodle or rice salads and grilled meats.

MAKES ABOUT ⅔ CUP

---

1 cup peeled and thinly sliced shallots (about 6 ounces)

1 cup vegetable oil

---

1. Line a tray or large plate with paper towels and spread the shallots on top. Let the shallots sit for 20 minutes to air-dry.

2. Heat the oil in a small skillet over medium-high heat. The oil will be ready when a piece of shallot slowly bubbles and floats to the top. Add the shallots and stir so that they do not tangle.

3. Fry the shallots, stirring frequently, until golden brown, about 5 minutes. Remove the shallots from the pan with a slotted spoon and drain on paper towels. You can save the oil for another use.

| Chef's Note |

using lemongrass

Lemongrass has a haunting citrus and spice effect and can be found in more and more markets. For using in a salad such as this, look for stalks with thick bulbs. Trim off the root end and peel back the tough outer layer. Thinly slice the bottom third of the stalk. The upper part of stalk is usually used to infuse soups and stocks and then discarded. If you are using only the lower part, tightly wrap the upper stalks and place in the freezer for up to 4 months.

cold orange chile oil noodle salad

This recipe is great for a party or just to have on hand when the days are hot and the noodles are cold. You can also toss in bits of leftover grilled chicken, pork, or beef.

From Adam Busby, director of education and Certified Master Chef.

2 tablespoons Orange Chile Oil (recipe follows)

1 tablespoon sediment from bottom of the Orange Chile Oil

2 tablespoons soy sauce

2 tablespoons white wine vinegar

1 teaspoon kosher salt, or as needed

1 tablespoon sugar

8 ounces fresh bean sprouts

1 pound very thin fresh Chinese noodles

¾ cup finely shredded carrots

¾ cup fresh cilantro leaves, plus as needed for garnish

½ cup chopped dry-roasted and salted peanuts

1. In a small bowl, combine the oil, oil sediment, soy sauce, vinegar, salt, and sugar and whisk to combine. Reserve until needed.

2. Bring a large pot of salted water to a boil over high heat. Have a bowl of ice water on hand (see page 41). Place the bean sprouts in a small colander that can be submerged in the pot. Submerge the bean sprouts in boiling water for 15 seconds. Drain and immediately place in the ice water until completely cool. Cover with ice-cold water and reserve in the refrigerator.

3. Bring the water in the pot back to a boil. Have another bowl of ice water on hand. Gently untangle the noodles and drop them into the boiling water. Cook, stirring occasionally, until just al dente, about 2 minutes. Drain, place in the ice water until completely cool, and drain well again. Place the noodles in a large bowl and refrigerate.

4. Just before serving, rewhisk the dressing, add to the noodles, and toss well to coat, gently separating the noodles as you toss.

5. Drain the bean sprouts well and add to the noodles, along with the carrots, cilantro leaves, and 6 tablespoons of the peanuts. Toss well to combine and coat the ingredients with the dressing. Place the noodle salad on a platter and garnish with the additional cilantro leaves and the remaining 2 tablespoons of chopped peanuts.

orange chile oil

You'll have extra oil, but it keeps in the refrigerator for at least a week. Use as a vinaigrette, to make an orange mayonnaise, or to create a room-temperature summer rice salad. The combination of peanut and canola oil is great, but you can use one or the other or a good-quality corn oil.

1 large orange (10 ounces)

1 to 2 tablespoons red pepper flakes, depending on desired heat

2 tablespoons Chinese black beans, coarsely chopped

1 teaspoon minced garlic

½ cup canola oil

½ cup peanut oil

2 teaspoons toasted sesame oil

1. Zest the orange in long strips, trying to get as little of the white pith as possible. Mince the peel and reserve the orange for another use.

2. In a small, heavy saucepan, combine the zest and the remaining ingredients. Bring the mixture to simmer over low heat and adjust the heat to keep at a very gentle simmer. Cook for 15 minutes, stirring occasionally. Cool and store in a covered container in the refrigerator.

sweet white corn soup with crab and chive oil

The first appearance of local sweet corn is the inspiration for this heavenly soup. This one should have you seeking picked-that-morning corn from your farmers' market or a nearby farm stand. The corn and crab complement each other, whereas the sweetness of the corn contrasts with the smokiness of the bacon, creating layer upon layer of savory late-summer flavors. The herbal undertones of the chive oil suggest the verdancy of the garden and the lightness that is life in the wine country in late summer.

SERVES 6

6 ears sweet corn (12 to 16 ounces each)

2 ounces applewood-smoked slab bacon, cut into thirds (about 2-inch pieces)

2 tablespoons butter

2 small onions (8 to 10 ounces each), peeled and cut into ¼-inch slices

10 sprigs fresh thyme

1 sprig fresh sage

6 cups chicken stock

1 ½ pounds Yukon gold potatoes, peeled and cut into ¼-inch slices

1 teaspoon kosher salt, or as needed

½ teaspoon freshly ground black pepper, or as needed

¾ cup heavy cream

4 ounces fresh Maine, rock, or peekytoe crabmeat or lobster meat

6 tablespoons Chive Oil (page 74)

1. Cut the kernels from the cobs. Reserve the kernels and two corncobs.

2. Place the bacon in a heavy-bottomed large soup pot over low heat and cook until the fat is rendered, about 4 minutes. Do not brown the bacon.

3. Increase the heat to medium-high and add the butter and onions to the pot. Sweat the onions until soft and translucent, 4 to 5 minutes.

4. Tie together the thyme and sage sprigs and add to the onion mixture.

5. Add the chicken stock, potatoes, and the reserved corncobs. Bring to a simmer over medium heat and season with salt and pepper. Simmer until the potatoes are cooked through, about 30 minutes.

6. Add the cream, stir to combine, and bring the soup to a boil. Reduce to a simmer, add the reserved kernels, and simmer for 5 minutes.

7. Remove the soup from the heat and discard the bacon, corncobs, and herb sprigs.

8. Blend the soup until smooth, 1 to 2 minutes. Adjust the seasoning with salt and pepper.

9. Pass the soup through a fine-mesh sieve into a saucepan and gently reheat.

10. Divide the soup among 6 soup bowls. Place about 2 tablespoons of the crab in each bowl and then drizzle about 1 tablespoon of chive oil over the crab. Serve immediately.

Wine Pairing

An off-dry sparkling wine will keep up with the sweetness of the corn and add an attractive texture to the creamy soup.

chive oil

Easy to make and the essence of summer, chive oil can also be used on tomato salads, grilled fish, over niçoise olives, and on couscous and other grain salads. The oil keeps in the refrigerator for 1 week.

MAKES ABOUT 1 CUP

---

2 bunches chives (about 1 ounce each)

1 cup olive oil

¼ teaspoon salt, or as needed

---

1. Place the chives, olive oil, and salt in a blender. Purée until smooth, about 30 seconds. Let sit overnight, covered, in a stainless-steel bowl.

2. Strain the purée through a fine-mesh sieve and store in a plastic squeeze bottle or small container in the refrigerator.

chilled yellow tomato soup with lemon balm and mint

The frostiest of soups for the hottest of days and meant for late summer, when the tomatoes are really ripe and sweet and juicy. Taste the tomato base before refrigerating or freezing it; add sugar if the tomatoes are not truly sweet, and if the tomatoes are really sweet, add a touch more vinegar. Keep in mind that by chilling and freezing the soup, you'll be tapping down the salty, sweet, and acidic flavors, so season with just slightly more of these elements than you will want in the finished soup.

SERVES 6

soup

4 pounds Golden Jubilee tomatoes or other yellow tomatoes

2 to 4 tablespoons Champagne vinegar, depending upon acidity of tomatoes

1 tablespoon sea salt, or as needed

¼ teaspoon freshly ground white pepper, or as needed

1 tablespoon fresh lime juice, or as needed

1 tablespoon sugar (optional), depending upon ripeness of tomatoes

garnishes

4 fresh lemon balm leaves

8 fresh mint leaves

4 fresh purple basil leaves

12 cherry tomatoes (about 3 ounces), washed and quartered

3 small tomatillos (about 3 ounces), husked, washed well, and quartered

1. Place 6 small soup bowls in the freezer.

2. For the soup: Wash the tomatoes and cut into eighths. Puree in a blender until smooth and strain through a fine-mesh sieve into a bowl. Add the vinegar, salt, white pepper, and lime juice. Taste and adjust the seasonings, adding sugar and vinegar if necessary.

3. Remove 2 cups of the soup and place in a small container or ice cube trays. Freeze for at least 4 hours. Refrigerate the rest of the soup.

4. Just before you're ready to serve, place the frozen soup in a food processor and pulse until the mixture has the consistency of crushed ice. Pour into a small bowl and place back in the freezer until ready to serve.

5. For the garnishes: Lay the herbs on top of each other. Roll into a cylinder and cut very thinly (chiffonade). Reserve until needed. Combine the cherry tomatoes and tomatillos. Reserve until needed.

6. Remove the chilled soup from the refrigerator and stir. Divide the tomato mixture among each of 6 bowls. Ladle a serving of soup (about 1 ¼ cups) on top of the tomatillo and cherry tomato pieces. Remove the frozen soup base from the freezer and scoop about 2 tablespoons into each soup using a 1-ounce scoop. Garnish with a heaping ½ teaspoon of the herbs and serve immediately.

Wine Pairing

Find a glorious vintage blanc de blancs sparkling wine to enjoy with this soup. The high acid and full flavors of both will make you feel refreshed.

frittata with goat cheese and green olives

Frittatas are a way to both grab produce that's at its peak or as a way to use up a bit of this and that left over from the week's kitchen adventures. It can be made in the cool of the day, refrigerated, and then served at room temperature with a small cold salad. Once you have the basics, it's a dish that can carry you through the seasons: sage, squash, and potatoes in fall; white beans and bits of meat in winter; and leftover pasta, peas, and asparagus in the spring.

SERVES 6 TO 8

2 **tablespoons** olive oil

1 **cup** finely diced white onion

2 small garlic cloves, peeled

2 **cups** thinly sliced pattypan or young yellow squash

10 eggs

½ **teaspoon** salt, or as needed

¼ **teaspoon** freshly ground black pepper, or as needed

2 **tablespoons** finely minced chives

3 **ounces** goat cheese, crumbled

6 thinly sliced green olives

6 **ounces** of cooked thinly sliced potatoes or cooked pasta (optional)

1. Preheat the oven to 400°F.

2. In a large ovenproof sauté pan, warm the olive oil over medium-high heat. Add the onion and garlic and sauté, stirring, until the onion is translucent, about 4 minutes. Add the squash and sauté just until soft, 4 to 5 minutes. Remove the garlic and discard. This will provide the dish with just a hint of garlic flavor.

3. Place the eggs in a medium bowl and whisk just until combined and a bit frothy. Add the eggs to the pan and swirl to mix with the other ingredients. Add the salt and pepper.

4. Sprinkle in the chives, goat cheese, olives, and potatoes (if using). Cook until the bottom of the frittata is just set, about 1 minute, then place the pan in the oven.

5. Bake until just set and firm to the touch, about 10 minutes. Loosen the edges of the frittata with a spatula and invert onto a plate or cutting board. Cut into 6 or 8 wedges and serve immediately or refrigerate until ready to use.

Wine Pairing

Whenever you have green olives, reach for a Rhône varietal rosé to complete transportation to the south of France.

eggplant sandwiches with tomato jam

Even for people who don't usually like eggplant (myself included), the new varieties of smaller Italian eggplants coming onto market are less bitter, and, in this recipe, their inherent smokiness contrasts perfectly with the creamy feta and tart tomato jam. I start looking for these often purple or purple-and-white-striped varieties at the Longmeadow Ranch stand at the farmers' market sometime in late July. However, if you can't find Italian eggplants, you can substitute a large globe eggplant. The sandwiches can be made in advance and then quickly sautéed as a last step. Wrapping the sandwiches in parchment paper makes them pickup and party ready.

MAKES 12 SANDWICHES; SERVES 6

4 tablespoons olive oil, or as needed

3 small Italian eggplants (6 to 8 ounces each), ends trimmed, cut into ½-inch slices (about 24 slices)

8 ounces feta cheese, French if available, cut into ¼-inch slices

3 eggs, beaten

1 cup fresh bread crumbs

½ teaspoon salt

1½ cups Tomato Jam (page 79)

1. In a large skillet over medium heat, warm 2 tablespoons of the oil. Fry the eggplant slices in two batches, turning once, until the slices are golden brown and softened, about 4 minutes per side. You may need to add a little more of the oil for the second batch. Drain the slices on a plate lined with paper towels.

2. Place a slice of the feta on half of the eggplant rounds, then top with the remaining rounds.

3. Dip each eggplant sandwich in the beaten egg, then coat with bread crumbs.

4. Heat the remaining olive oil in the skillet over medium heat and gently sauté the eggplant sandwiches, covered, until the cheese melts and the crust is golden brown, 2 to 3 minutes per side. Drain on a plate lined with paper towels.

5. Salt the eggplant sandwiches, place on individual plates or a platter, and serve immediately with tomato jam.

Wine Pairing

Try these with a young, simple Sangiovese to match the full flavors of salty eggplant and cheese.

tomato jam

You'll have more tomato jam than you need for the eggplant sandwiches, but it keeps, covered, in the refrigerator for up to 2 weeks.

MAKES ABOUT 2 CUPS

2 tablespoons olive oil

1 onion, cut into ¼-inch dice

2 garlic cloves, peeled and crushed

2 tablespoons tomato paste

4 large tomatoes (about 2½ pounds), preferably heirlooms, cored and coarsely chopped

2 tablespoons balsamic vinegar

1 sprig fresh rosemary

1 teaspoon kosher salt, or as needed

½ teaspoon freshly ground black pepper, or as needed

1. In a large skillet, heat the olive oil over medium-high heat. Add the onion and garlic and sauté until the onion is translucent, about 5 minutes. Remove and discard the garlic.

2. Add the tomato paste and fry, stirring, until the tomato paste just begins to caramelize, about 2 minutes. Add the tomatoes, vinegar, and rosemary and simmer, uncovered, for about 20 minutes, stirring frequently to keep the tomatoes from sticking to the bottom of the pan, until the tomatoes are virtually dry and have a jamlike consistency.

3. Season the jam with salt and pepper and remove the rosemary sprig.

fresh pasta with summer herbs, fresh ricotta, and roasted tomato coulis

Seven terraces of organic culinary herbs sweep up the front of Greystone, where early in the morning, you can find flocks of chefs picking basil and tarragon and thyme to accent the day's dishes. The heady seduction of just-plucked herbs and the profusion of summer tomatoes are the inspiration for this pasta dish, created by chef-instructor Lars Kronmark.

More complex than a raw tomato concoction and less serious than a long-simmered sauce, the roasted tomato coulis has a harvest feel, with the addition of fresh ricotta at the end adding just a touch of creaminess. Tossing the linguine with the barely braised herbs releases their sun-soaked fragrances, and the addition of sea salt and olive oil lends an elegant finish.

The coulis can be made in advance and reheated as needed. See the following Chef's Note for additional coulis information.

MAKES **6** GENEROUS FIRST-COURSE SERVINGS

roasted tomato coulis

3 tablespoons extra-virgin olive oil

3 pounds ripe, preferably heirloom, tomatoes, cut in half and most of liquid and seeds squeezed out

2 garlic cloves, peeled

2 shallots, peeled

2 celery stalks, cut in large chunks

½ cup vegetable or chicken stock, or as needed

1 teaspoon kosher salt, or as needed

½ teaspoon freshly ground black pepper, or as needed

pasta and herbs

3 tablespoons fruity, good-quality extra-virgin olive oil

2 cloves garlic, minced

1 cup Chardonnay

1 pound fresh linguine

¼ cup finely minced fresh chives

¼ cup finely chopped basil

¼ cup finely chopped fresh flat-leaf parsley

2 tablespoons finely chopped fresh tarragon

2 tablespoons finely chopped fresh dill

8 ounces fresh ricotta

1½ teaspoons coarse sea salt, or as needed

1. Preheat the oven to 400°F.

2. For the tomato coulis: Toss 2 tablespoons of the olive oil, the tomatoes, garlic, shallots, and celery together and place on a baking sheet with sides. Roast in the oven, shaking the pan occasionally to prevent sticking, until the tomatoes begin to caramelize, about 20 minutes.

3. Remove the pan from the oven and purée the roasted vegetables and their accumulated liquids in a blender, adding the stock as necessary to achieve a smooth, loose, pestolike consistency.

4. Add the remaining tablespoon of olive oil, the salt, and pepper and blend for a few more seconds to combine thoroughly. Strain the coulis through a fine-mesh sieve and keep warm.

5. For the pasta: In a large sauté pan, warm 2 tablespoons of the olive oil over medium heat. Add the garlic, cover, and sweat until the garlic is softened, about 1 minute. Increase the heat to medium-high and add the wine. Reduce the wine by half, 4 to 5 minutes. Remove from the heat and reserve.

6. Bring a pot of well-salted water to a boil over high heat and cook the pasta until al dente, about 2 minutes.

7. Drain the pasta and place in the sauté pan with the wine. Heat over medium heat, tossing to coat the pasta, until well combined and heated through. Add the chives, basil, parsley, tarragon, and dill and toss to coat the pasta. Pour about ½ to ¾ cup of tomato coulis on each of 6 warmed dishes and divide the pasta among the dishes.

8. With two soup spoons, scoop out about 1½ tablespoons of ricotta from its container and pass between spoons, forming an oval shape. Place the shaped ricotta on top of the pasta.

9. Drizzle each mound of ricotta with ½ teaspoon of the remaining olive oil and sprinkle with about ¼ teaspoon coarse sea salt. Encourage your guests to mix the pasta with the coulis and ricotta.

Wine Pairing

Chef Kronmark recommends a Chardonnay pairing to reflect the Chardonnay used in the recipe.

| Chef's Note |

coulis

A coulis is a thick purée, usually made of vegetables, but possibly of fruit. By roasting the vegetables, the acidity of the tomatoes is reduced and the sweetness is increased, while the flavors in general become more concentrated.

Technique:
grilling

Keeping foods moist while infusing them with the flavors of smoke and wood is the pursuit of all outdoor cooks. Dry rubs, brining, cedar planks, and tongs are a few ways to ensure that you get that perfect contrast of crispy crust and juiciness that is the hallmark of the grill master.

dry rubs

Found in many traditional cuisines around the world, dry spice rubs are seasoning blends used to flavor and tenderize poultry, meats, and fish. Rubs work by drawing a portion of the meat juices to the surface, where they mingle with the seasoning to form a thin layer, or crust, that seals in the remaining juices and the flavor.

Sprinkle rubs over meat, poultry, fish, or veggies and lightly rub into the surface with your hands. You can also place the rub in a large plastic bag, add your ingredients, and shake to coat. Three to four tablespoons of spice rub seasonings should be enough for two pounds of food. Let sit in the refrigerator for several hours or overnight. Shake off the excess dry rub or paste before grilling. Grill using direct heat on a lightly oiled rack until done.

brining

Brining uses osmosis—and salt, sugar and water—to "pull" impurities out of meat and then "push" moisture and flavors back in. Many cuts of pork benefit from brining, as do whole chickens and turkeys that are less than 18 pounds.

See the recipe on page 96 for a brining liquid for pork chops. For whole chickens and turkeys, a general rule of thumb is to use 1 cup kosher salt and ½ cup sugar to 1 gallon of water or use a pre-prepared brining mix and brine in the refrigerator overnight.

cedar planks

Used by Native Americans of the Pacific Northwest for cooking salmon, cedar planks infuse foods with the subtle flavor of cedar and a mild smokiness, while keeping fish, chicken, duck, and pork extremely moist.

When using cedar planks, be sure to follow the directions that come with them. Always use caution while grilling with a plank. Heavy-duty oven mitts and long tongs should be used when moving the plank and food on and off the grill.

Prior to using a plank, you'll need to soak it in water to create steam and to keep the plank itself from charring once it is exposed to heat. Soak it in water for at least 1 hour or up to 24 hours. When you are ready to grill, build a fire that places the coals on either side of the grill, creating an open slot in the middle of the grill. Or place all the coals to one side, leaving the other side empty. Place a piece of aluminum over the place where there are no coals (where there is indirect heat). Place the plank on the aluminum foil and preheat, turning every couple of minutes. Place the food directly onto the plank and cover the grill. Grill until the food is done, without turning.

use tongs

Use tongs instead of a barbecue fork or even a knife, as forks and knives poke holes in the meat that can allow juices to drain out.

allow the meat to "rest"

When you grill a piece of meat, the muscle fibers contract and drive the juices to the center of the cut. Meat served right off the grill can taste tough and dry, but a post-grill rest allows the muscle fibers to reabsorb juices, with more tender and succulent results. Resting the meat for 10 minutes, loosely tented with aluminum foil to retain heat, works for most cuts.

fish tacos with citrus-cucumber relish and pico de gallo

Yes, it is true. We do drink beer here. Especially on those really hot days and especially if we've been out in the vineyards. And on those 100°F-plus days, when looking for foods that refresh, for something made with produce from the farmers' market in August, and absolutely no time with anything hot in the kitchen, fish tacos come to mind.

We have serious debates in these parts about just what constitutes a classic fish taco. Fried vs. grilled fish? Red cabbage vs. green? Whatever the details, there are four basic parts: the fish, slaw (in the recipe below, a close cousin, cucumber relish, is used), pico de gallo, and *crema* or sour cream.

Purists insist that pico de gallo be used in fish tacos, as it is typically has less liquid than its salsa sister. Making a paste of the garlic and salt takes off some of the raw garlic's edge and allows it to blend more easily with the other flavors.

MAKES 12 TACOS; SERVES 6

marinade

⅓ **cup** olive oil

2 **tablespoons** fresh lime juice

1 **teaspoon** ancho chile powder

1½ **pounds** halibut, cut into six 4-ounce pieces

cucumber-citrus relish

½ English cucumber (about 8 ounces), thinly sliced

½ red onion (about 8 ounces), peeled and cut into thin strips

1 **tablespoon plus** ½ **teaspoon** salt, or as needed

1 **teaspoon** minced serrano chile

2 **tablespoons** fresh orange juice

2 **tablespoons** fresh lime juice

1 **teaspoon** sugar, or as needed

¼ **teaspoon** freshly ground black pepper

pico de gallo

1 **teaspoon** minced garlic

1 **teaspoon** salt, or as needed

1½ **pounds** ripe Roma tomatoes, seeded and cut into ¼-inch dice

¼ **cup** finely diced red onion

1 small jalapeño chile, stemmed, seeded, deribbed, and minced

1 **tablespoon** red wine vinegar

1 **tablespoon** olive oil

¼ **cup** coarsely chopped fresh cilantro

crema

¼ **cup** low-fat mayonnaise

¼ **cup** low-fat sour cream

2 **tablespoons** fresh lime juice

Twelve 5-inch corn tortillas

[recipe continues]

1. For the marinade: Mix all of the ingredients together in a shallow dish. Thirty minutes before grilling, toss the fish with the marinade and allow to marinate in the refrigerator.

2. For the cucumber-citrus relish: Sprinkle the cucumber and onion with the 1 tablespoon salt and place in a colander in the sink or over a bowl for 30 minutes to drain excess water.

3. Just before serving, in a medium bowl, combine the cucumber-onion mixture with the rest of the relish ingredients and adjust the seasoning with the ½ teaspoon salt and pepper.

4. For the pico de gallo: Place the minced garlic on a cutting board and sprinkle the salt over the garlic. Using the flat part of a chef's knife, comb the salt through the garlic to make a paste. Reserve in a medium bowl. Just before serving, add in the rest of the ingredients and refrigerate until needed.

5. For the *crema*: Mix together the mayonnaise, sour cream, and lime juice and refrigerate until needed.

6. Light a charcoal fire or turn a gas grill to medium-high heat. Brush the grill grate with oil. Grill the fish with a bit of marinade still clinging to it until just opaque in the center, 3 to 5 minutes on each side.

7. Warm the corn tortillas on the grill for about 20 seconds on each side and then wrap in aluminum foil. Keep the tortillas warm off the direct heat on the grill.

8. Spoon about 2 heaping tablespoons of the cucumber relish along the center of each tortilla. Divide each 4-ounce piece of fish in half and flake each half onto a tortilla. Spoon about 2 heaping tablespoons of pico de gallo on top of the fish. Drizzle with about 2 teaspoons of the *crema*. Fold the tortillas in half and serve.

grilled brined shrimp with tomatillo-and-avocado salsa

Relaxing outside is the mantra of this recipe: You can make the salsa while the shrimp are marinating, and all that's left to deliver dinner is to quickly cook the shrimp for just a few minutes on the grill. Brining helps create a moist, salty smokiness in the grilled shrimp, which plays well with the refreshing citrus-like tartness of the tomatillos and richness of the avocado.

From faculty member and Live Fire Workshop grill man John Ash.

SERVES 4

brine

⅓ **cup** kosher salt

⅓ **cup** packed brown sugar

1 quart cold water

1 pound large shrimp (21/30 count), peeled and deveined

marinade

¼ **cup** olive oil

2 teaspoons finely chopped garlic

1 tablespoon chopped fresh flat-leaf parsley

¼ **teaspoon** red pepper flakes, or as needed

2 tablespoons dry white wine

tomatillo-and-avocado salsa

4 ounces fresh tomatillos, husked, washed, and coarsely chopped

1 teaspoon chopped garlic

1 teaspoon coarsely chopped serrano chile, or as needed

1 large ripe avocado (about 12 ounces), peeled, pitted, and coarsely chopped

1 tablespoon chopped green onion

2 tablespoons extra-virgin olive oil

1 tablespoon fresh lemon juice

½ **teaspoon** kosher salt, or as needed

¼ **teaspoon** freshly ground black pepper, or as needed

2 tablespoons coarsely chopped fresh cilantro

1. For the brine: Stir all of the ingredients together until the salt and sugar dissolve. Add the shrimp and refrigerate for up to an hour.

2. For the marinade: Mix all of the ingredients together in a small bowl and set aside.

3. Remove the shrimp from the brine and rinse thoroughly. Toss with the marinade, coat, and marinate for up to 1 hour in the refrigerator.

4. For the salsa: In a food processor, combine the tomatillos, garlic, and chile and pulse to finely chop. Add the avocado and green onion and pulse until just blended. You can also do this step by hand, finely chopping the tomatillos, garlic, and chile, placing the mixture in a bowl, and folding in the avocado and green onion. The salsa should have a bit of texture.

5. Place the salsa in a small bowl and toss with the olive oil, lemon juice, salt, and pepper. Store, covered and refrigerated, for up to 2 hours. Toss with the cilantro just before serving.

6. Light a charcoal fire. Drain the shrimp from the marinade. Grill the shrimp on both sides over medium-hot coals until they are just cooked through, about 3 minutes total, turning halfway through. Place the shrimp on plates and top with the salsa. Serve warm or at room temperature.

Wine Pairing

The shrimp's sweetness and the buttery but acid-laced salsa call for a crisp, clean, and palate cleansing white wine like an unoaked Sauvignon Blanc or Pinot Gris/Grigio or a dry Riesling.

cedar-roasted salmon with tomato-endive salad

Cooking the salmon fillets on cedar planks keeps the fish very moist while giving it a fresh, fir-forest fragrance and an earthy, wood-smoke allure. The refreshing crunch of the endive contrasts with the soft tomatoes, and the citrus and mustard vinaigrette cuts through the richness of the salmon.

Adapted from a recipe taught by Chef Lars Kronmark in CIA Greystone's Charcuterie, Smokehouse, and Condiment Workshop professional development class.

SERVES 6

fish

3 tablespoons fresh lemon juice

3 tablespoons Dijon mustard

3 tablespoons honey

¼ cup extra-virgin olive oil

6 salmon fillets (about 6 ounces each), skin and bones removed, wild if available

salad

2 tablespoons fresh lemon juice

2 tablespoons red wine vinegar

1 teaspoon minced garlic

2 tablespoons minced fresh basil leaves

½ cup extra-virgin olive oil

½ teaspoon kosher salt, or as needed

¼ teaspoon freshly ground black pepper, or as needed

1 tablespoon chopped fresh flat-leaf parsley

1½ cups halved cherry tomatoes

3 Belgium endives (2 to 3 ounces each), thinly sliced

2 cups frisée or watercress leaves

1. For the fish: Prepare two cedar planks (see page 82).

2. In a bowl, combine the lemon juice, mustard, honey, and olive oil. Add the fillets to the marinade, coating both sides, and marinate for 20 minutes in the refrigerator.

3. Cook the salmon according to directions that come with the plank, about 20 minutes.

4. While the salmon is cooking, start the salad. In a medium bowl, whisk together the lemon juice, vinegar, garlic, and basil. Allow the mixture to sit for 10 minutes. Whisk in the olive oil and season with the salt and pepper. Stir in the parsley. Place the cherry tomatoes, endives, and frisée in a medium bowl.

5. Just before the fish is ready, toss the salad with half of vinaigrette and add more as needed.

6. Carefully remove the salmon fillets from the planks, place each fillet on a serving plate, and spoon a generous cup of the salad around each serving. Serve immediately.

Wine Pairing

An oaky Chardonnay with plenty of acid complements the woody notes you get from the cedar but is also bright enough to match the freshness of the salad.

sauvignon blanc

For an adult, the first sip of cold Sauvignon Blanc at the end of a hot, hazy summer day brings the same satisfaction as drinking cold lemonade on the back porch. Cooling, acidic, and citrusy with a fruity core that reminds us of our childhood warm-weather treats, Sauvignon Blanc actually helps make us grateful for the long days—scorching or not—that allow us to enjoy the bounty of the garden and the grill.

what is sauvignon blanc?

Sauvignon Blanc is best known in its French incarnations as Sancerre from the Loire Valley, or Graves or other white Bordeaux. More recently, the exuberant offerings from Southern Hemisphere wine regions like New Zealand, Chile, and South Africa have grabbed the world's attention, and the grape's ability to express any number of styles in California makes it a highly desirable venture for innumerable winemakers here. A wide range of bottlings, from the clean, lemony wines of the Loire to the rich, elegant versions in Bordeaux and the lively wines of Marlborough, New Zealand, are likely to be conjured up in amazingly similar likenesses here in the Golden State. It seems now there are as many styles of Sauvignon Blanc, or "SB" as they like to say in the business, as fish in the ocean. The choices that determine these styles seem infinite.

styles of sauvignon blanc

Sauvignon Blanc can be fermented in either stainless-steel tanks or barrels—and sometimes the finished wines are a blend of the two. If you ferment in stainless steel, the Sauvignon Blanc will have very clean, fresh flavors, like plain, pure, ripe lemon juice. Fermenting in the barrel will give broader, more expansive, lush features to the wine; it's like the difference between lemon juice and lemon curd. Winemakers sometimes use malolactic fermentation, a process often used with Chardonnay to make buttery flavors, to round out the palate of SBs, lower the prickly acids, and turn that lemon into lemon cream. Oak would add another dimension and depth of flavor, now moving in the lemon-pound-cake direction, with subtle vanilla flavors and a round, substantial, mouth-filling wine.

While the natural character of the grape should lead to a few basic flavor components, such as floral, fruity, and subtly green, most California SBs will fall into one of these three categories. First there's lean, minerally, and blazing with acidity. Almost austere and reminiscent of many old-world versions of the grape, wines like these come mostly from cooler appellations in the state. Secondly, there's a popular style that's light, crisp, slightly fruity, and with a graceful acidity. Look for a little more range in these stylish wines, from citrus fruits and herb aromas to passion fruit and pineapple, with sometimes surprising green aromas. Finally, we're lucky to have in California a rich, round style of SB, layered with fruit, spice, and touches of toast and vanilla. This wine, usually in small production, often wisely blends the fruit with a touch of Semillon, another grape variety used in classic Graves from Bordeaux, and oak used in its proper perspective. This last category of wines are among the most serious Sauvignon Blancs made in the world.

sauvignon blanc and food

Just as the crisp white shirt or little black dress are must-haves in the closet, Sauvignon Blanc in whatever style you choose is now the classic essential for the American dinner table. High-acid wines at the table are superb for their ability to whet our appetite and brighten the flavors of many different types of dishes, much in the same way that a squeeze of lemon and a pinch of salt can take food from ho-hum to hidy-hidy-ho! In fact, ask any sommelier what the one crucial component in wine is that makes it a great "food wine" they'd say without hesitation, "Acid."

With the abundant flavors of summer, the possibilities for bringing Sauvignon Blanc to the table are huge. With salads, no matter what the ingredients, be sure to include an SB with a good dose of acid, a citrus core, and a flinty mineral finish to pair with your vinaigrette. In the height of summer, when produce is ripe, plentiful, and sweet, look for SBs that have the same flavor profile for sweet tomatoes, grilled peaches, melon salads, roasted peppers, and zucchini. Even when you dust off the grill, don't discount a Sauvignon Blanc—with barbecued shrimp or smoky chicken sausage, an oaked Fumé-style Sauvignon Blanc with its spicy, puckery Pippin-apple finish is an ideal accompaniment.

storage and serving

In a nutshell: Most Sauvignon Blancs are best in their youth, though some styles can age for a few years, and are best enjoyed chilled.

spottswoode paella

Every summer, Beth Novak Milliken and her husband, John Milliken, host a backyard paella-on-the-grill bash for about fifty friends across from Spottswoode, the Novak's family winery and one of Napa Valley's most beautifully gardened properties. Cooking paella on the grill or over a fire on the beach can be a summer tradition for you, too. It's great for a party: Much can be done in advance, such as chopping the onions and tomatoes and blanching the beans, and if you have everything measured out and ready to go, it's a hang-around-the-fire sort of group activity. You can get guests involved, peeling the charred peppers, tending the fire, making sure the cook has a glass of wine in hand. Started as a way to feed hungry field workers in Spain, there are as many versions of paella as there are people who cook it. This one omits the chicken thighs that are often included. Add boiled lobster with the shellfish toward the end of the cooking time if it's around and you're feeling flush. Ideally, there will be a thin, golden crust called a *soccorat* that has formed on the bottom of the pan when the paella is done, but this can be tricky for paella novices, as the rice on the bottom can very quickly begin to burn. After the rice has cooked more or less halfway through, begin to scrape up a bit of the bottom layer of the rice from the center of the pan to make sure it is not blackening. If it is, turn the heat down or move the pan to a cooler part of the grill.

SERVES 8 TO 10, GENEROUSLY

1 teaspoon saffron threads	2 red bell peppers (about 8 ounces each)
3 cups Sauvignon Blanc	½ **cup** olive oil
2 tablespoons chopped fresh flat-leaf parsley	**1 pound** large shrimp (21/30 count), in shell
1 small shallot (1 ounce), minced	3 Spanish chorizo sausages (about 12 ounces total), cut into ½-inch pieces
12 ounces small mussels	8 garlic cloves, peeled and very thinly sliced
12 ounces small clams, such as manilas or cherrystones	**1 tablespoon** pimentón (Spanish paprika)
2 onions (about 8 ounces each), peeled and coarsely chopped	**3 cups** good-quality rice, such as Bomba or Valencia
2 tomatoes (about 12 ounces to 1 pound), halved, seeded, and coarsely chopped	**Two** 4-inch sprigs fresh rosemary
6 cups good-quality, well-salted chicken stock, or as needed	3 lemons, cut into eighths
8 ounces Italian green beans	1 bunch green onions, trimmed and sliced very thinly

1. Toast the saffron threads in a small saucepan over medium heat, stirring or shaking the pan constantly until the saffron is fragrant, about 2 minutes. Add 1½ cups of the wine, bring to a boil, then adjust the heat so that the liquid is at a simmer. Simmer until the wine is deeply colored, about 3 minutes. Remove from the heat and reserve until needed.

2. Place the remaining 1½ cups wine, the parsley, and shallot in a large skillet. Bring to a simmer over medium-high heat. Add the mussels and clams, cover the pan, and steam, shaking the pan often, until they just begin to open, 3 to 4 minutes. Discard any clams or mussels that do not open. Drain the shellfish in a fine-mesh sieve lined with cheesecloth into a large bowl. Reserve the liquid and shellfish (refrigerate both if not using right away).

3. Place the onions in a food processor and pulse until coarsely grated, about 8 pulses. Remove from the food processor and place in a small bowl. Reserve until needed. Place the tomatoes in the food processor and pulse until coarsely grated, about 8 pulses. Remove from the food processor and place in a small bowl. Reserve until needed.

4. In a medium saucepan, bring the chicken stock to a simmer over medium-high heat. Remove from heat and reserve warm until needed.

5. Bring a large pot of well-salted water to a boil. Have a bowl of ice water on hand (see page 41). Add the green beans and blanch until bright green, about 1 minute. Remove and immediately place in ice water to stop the cooking. Drain, cut in half, and reserve until needed.

6. Prepare the grill. Wood is ideal, charcoal briquettes are fine, and a gas grill turned to high will do. When very hot, char the red peppers on all sides, about 4 minutes per side. Place in a paper bag, close, and let the peppers steam until their skin loosens and they are easily handled, about 15 minutes. With a paring knife, scrape off the blackened skin, remove the seeds and ribs, and cut the peppers into ¼-inch strips. Reserve until needed.

7. Place a 15-inch paella pan over the hot fire. Add the olive oil and warm until a sheen develops on the oil, about 1 minute. Add the shrimp and sauté, stirring frequently, until they just turn pink and shrink a bit, about 2 minutes. Remove from the pan and reserve. Add the sausages and sauté, stirring frequently, until just browned, about 2 minutes. Remove from the pan and reserve with the shrimp. Do not overcook the shrimp or the sausages, as they will be added back to paella later to cook a bit more.

8. To make the *sofrito*, or flavor base, add the garlic and reserved grated onion to the paella pan and cook, stirring often, until the onion is just translucent, about 5 minutes. Add the reserved tomato pulp and cook, stirring often, until most of the moisture has cooked out, 5 to 7 minutes. Stir in the pimentón and rice and cook until the rice is translucent, about 2 minutes.

9. Get the fire burning really hot before adding the liquids. The Millikens use grapevine cuttings from the Spottswoode vineyard. You can use dry twigs or extra briquettes. Add the reserved warm saffron infusion, shellfish liquor, and all but 1 cup of the stock to the pan. Scatter the shrimp and sausage pieces over the rice, stir to combine, and bring the liquid to a boil. Adjust the heat or move the pan around (with oven mitts!) so that the liquid settles into a gentle simmer. Rotate the pan every 4 minutes or so for even heat distribution.

10. After about 15 to 20 minutes, the rice should start to emerge from the liquid. When all of the liquid is below the level of the rice, taste a piece of rice in the center of the pan midway from top to bottom for doneness. If the rice is still really undercooked, add a bit more warmed stock. Place the reserved mussels and clams hinge-side down over the rice and scatter the shrimp, beans, and red peppers over the paella, along with the rosemary. Cook for 3 to 4 more minutes, until all of the liquid is absorbed. Remove the pan from the heat, then cover the pan with aluminum foil. Let the paella rest for 5 minutes, uncover, and serve immediately with lemon wedges and green onions.

Wine Pairing

The most important wine advice for a paella dinner is to match the wine to the protein you're using. Lots of shellfish? Pick a high-acid white. If you tend toward a meatier dish, move into the reds. Either way, a little oak won't hurt because of the smoky essence of the classic preparation.

brined pork chops with red onion confit

If you've given up on cooking often-too-lean pork on the grill because of the cardboard-like results, try brining. It will increase both moisture and flavor in the pork. Searching out heritage breeds such as the Duroc will put pork back on the grilling menu.

SERVES 4

brine

6 cups cold water

1 bay leaf

¾ cup kosher salt

½ cup packed brown sugar

8 black peppercorns

6 allspice berries

6 garlic cloves, peeled and smashed

4 pork loin rib chops (about 3 pounds), bone in and cut 1½ to 2 inches thick

dry rub

1 tablespoon ground cumin

1 tablespoon chili powder

1 tablespoon curry powder

2 teaspoons brown sugar

1 teaspoon freshly ground black pepper

½ cup Red Onion Confit (facing page)

1. For the brine: Place all of the ingredients in a large saucepan and bring to a boil over high heat. Adjust the heat until the mixture is at a simmer. Simmer for 5 minutes. Cool completely.

2. Place the pork chops in the cold brine and marinate overnight.

3. For the dry rub: Combine all of the ingredients thoroughly.

4. After taking the chops out of the brine, dry them well with paper towels. Coat with the dry rub.

5. Prepare the grill using the "two-level" method: Spread half of the lit coals out into a single layer and leave the remaining coals in a pile to create two different sections of heat. The single layer is the medium-high heat, and the area with a couple of layers of coals is the high-heat side. Start by searing the chops over high heat until the outside has caramelized slightly, 2 to 3 minutes per side. Move the chops to the lower heat to cook more slowly, and cover the grill. Grill, turning once, until an instant-read thermometer inserted into the side of a pork chop away from the bone registers 135°F, 7 to 9 minutes longer. Let rest for 5 minutes, covered with foil (the internal temperature should rise to 145°F).

6. Serve each pork chop with about 2 tablespoons of red onion confit.

red onion confit

This recipe can easily be doubled and used with any number of grilled meats, such as sausages, hamburgers, and chicken.

MAKES ABOUT 1 CUP

2 tablespoons butter

1 quart chopped red onions (2 large, about 1 pound)

2 tablespoons honey

6 tablespoons red wine vinegar

6 tablespoons red wine

½ teaspoon kosher salt, or as needed

Freshly ground white pepper, as needed

1. Place the butter in a large sauté pan and melt over medium heat. Add the onions, cover, and, stirring frequently, cook until the onions have softened and begun to turn translucent but not browned, about 5 to 7 minutes.

2. Uncover, stir in the honey, turn the heat to medium-high, and continue to cook the onions, stirring often, until lightly caramelized, about 5 minutes.

3. Add the vinegar and red wine (be careful not to let the vinegar spatter). Simmer the mixture until the liquid is almost dry, stirring frequently to scrape the browned juices from the bottom of pan, about 5 minutes. Season with salt and pepper and reserve until needed.

Wine Pairing

A young, lighter-styled, fruity Syrah or Grenache would be wonderful with the lean, spice-rubbed meat.

summer fruit tart with lemon curd

After you've had your fill of fruit out of hand, sweeten things up a bit by taking berries and stone fruit to the next level. Less boisterous than their pie cousins, fruit tarts delicately express whatever fruit is most seasonal and at hand. There are four basic components of a fruit tart: the dough, a filling, the fruit, and usually a glaze. Once you learn the fundamentals, making one is a relatively easy skill that you can use throughout the year as peaches and blueberries give way to the apples and pears of fall (including the deeply caramelized appeal of tarte Tatins), then winter citrus and pineapple and on to spring strawberries. Although nothing is as good as from scratch, in the proverbial pinch you can use store-bought lemon curd. Make the tart dough in the cool of the morning. The dough will keep in the refrigerator for up to 5 days and will freeze for up to 1 month. Plenty of time to bring home some more fruit before it is gone until next year! "Arranging the fruit in a tart is where the art comes in," notes baking and pastry chef–instructor John DiFilippo. "Glazing is essential if fruit is cut, optional if left whole, although I like a combination of glazed and unglazed fruit in the same tart."

MAKES ONE 10-INCH TART; SERVES 8

1 pound Sweet Tart Dough (page 100)

lemon curd

2 large eggs

2 large egg yolks

¾ cup sugar

2 teaspoons finely grated lemon zest

¾ cup fresh lemon juice

½ cup butter, softened

1½ to 2 pounds stone fruit, depending upon the fruit (see Chef's Note page 100)

3 tablespoons apricot jam

1 to 2 tablespoons water

Fresh lemon verbena or mint leaves, for garnish (optional)

1. Preheat the oven to 350°F.

2. Allow the chilled dough to soften just until it indents easily from gentle finger pressure.

3. Place the disk on a lightly floured surface and dust a small amount of flour over the dough. Roll out the dough to a round about 11 inches in diameter. If the dough begins to stick, dust the work surface with a little more flour.

4. Invert the dough onto a 10-inch tart pan, press the dough into the corners, and trim off any excess that rises above the pan walls. Place in the freezer for 10 minutes before baking.

5. Remove the tart shell from the freezer and poke holes in the sides and bottom of the dough. Line the tart shell with parchment paper or aluminum foil and add enough pie weights or dried beans to fill the shell one-third to one-half full. Bake until the edges begin to look dry, 12 to 15 minutes. Remove the pan from the oven and then remove the weights and paper or foil. Return the pan to the oven and bake until the edges just start to turn brown, 8 to 10 minutes. Remove the shell from the oven and allow to cool completely before adding the lemon curd.

6. For the lemon curd: In a medium mixing bowl, whisk the eggs, egg yolks, sugar, lemon zest, and lemon juice together until smooth. Transfer the mixture to a double boiler (see page 201) over medium heat. Stirring continuously, cook the lemon mixture over simmering water until very thick, about 10 minutes. Add the softened butter and continue to whisk until the butter is blended in well.

[recipe continues]

7. Pour the lemon curd through a fine-mesh sieve into a clean bowl and cool over an ice bath.

8. When the curd is cooled but still not set, pour and spread evenly into the tart shell. Refrigerate the tart for at least 1 hour.

9. Slice and arrange the fruit on top of the lemon curd.

10. In a small saucepan over medium heat, warm the apricot jam and water and stir to create a smooth consistency. Remove from heat and, using a pastry brush, brush over the fruit.

11. Place the tart back in refrigerator to firm up. Garnish with verbena leaves if you like. Cut into 8 slices and serve.

Wine Pairing

Four words: *Late-Harvest Sauvignon Blanc*, especially if you're making this with peaches, nectarines, or apricots. The flavors of the fruit and wine will harmonize like the Drifters on a hot summer night. Make sure to pay attention to the sweetness levels when constructing your tart to pair with the wine. Too much sweetness in the tart will make the wine taste sour and vice versa. But what this really means is that you get to taste the wine before dessert!

sweet tart dough

MAKES ONE 10-INCH TART (ABOUT 14 OUNCES OF DOUGH)

½ **cup** cold, unsalted butter, cut into ¾-inch cubes

⅓ **cup** sugar

¼ **teaspoon** salt

1 large egg yolk

½ **teaspoon** vanilla extract

1¼ **cups** all-purpose flour

2 to 3 **tablespoons** ice water

---

1. In the bowl of an electric mixer fitted with the paddle attachment, cream together the butter, sugar, and salt until smooth and light in color, 2 to 3 minutes, scraping down the sides of the bowl as necessary. Add the egg yolk and vanilla and mix until smooth, 1 to 2 minutes more.

2. Add the flour all at once and mix until just blended, about 1 minute. Add the ice water 1 tablespoon at a time while the mixer is running; add just enough so that the dough comes together.

3. Turn the dough onto a lightly floured surface, gently pat into a disc, and wrap tightly with plastic wrap. Refrigerate until well chilled, about 30 minutes. If refrigerating for longer than 30 minutes, allow the dough to soften just enough that it can be indented with your finger.

| Chef's Note |

using stone fruit

Stone fruits cut in thin slices, such as nectarines, peaches, plums, and apricots, can be used on their own (often slightly overlapped in concentric circles), or in combination with raspberries, blueberries, strawberries, and blackberries. If cut into thin wedges, it's not necessary to take the skin off of stone fruits. Tossing it with a small amount of lemon juice will keep fruit from browning.

peach upside-down cake with raspberry sauce

I pass a small peach orchard almost every day, a small interlude between the vineyards and the Napa River. It is quiet most of the year, its trees a reminder of the valley's orchard-filled past. But sometime in early July, the orchard's "Peaches" sign announces the stand's opening "Next Sunday." I stop by a couple of times a week as a cascading series of catchy peach names—Suncrest, Flavorcrest, Babcock, and then Zee Lady and O'Henry—make their brief appearance in just over a few weeks. Each variety has its own drippingly good flavor and purpose—some for eating out of hand, others are best in pies, and yet some more for preserving.

This recipe, from Annie Baker, pastry chef at Napa Valley's iconic Mustards Restaurant and graduate of Greystone's Baking and Pastry Arts program, makes good use of the local peaches and the raspberries that are abundant this time of year. The richness and slightly smoky sweetness of the caramel plays well with the tart raspberries and juicy peaches.

You'll have extra raspberry sauce, which can be served over ice cream or added to yogurt. Please note that you'll need eight 10-ounce soufflé ramekins.

MAKES 8 INDIVIDUAL CAKES

---

3 cups fresh raspberries

1¼ cups granulated sugar, or to taste

1 tablespoon plus ¾ cup butter, softened, plus **1 cup**, melted

1½ cups packed light brown sugar

4 peaches (about 8 ounces each), halved and pitted

2 cups cake flour

1½ teaspoons baking powder

¼ teaspoon kosher salt

1 teaspoon vanilla extract

1 teaspoon almond extract

⅔ cup heavy cream

4 egg yolks

---

1. Preheat the oven to 350°F.

2. Purée the raspberries with ¼ cup of the granulated sugar in a food processor or blender until smooth, about 1 minute. Strain through a fine-mesh sieve, pushing the liquids through the solids, into a small bowl. Reserve at room temperature until needed.

3. Lightly butter eight 10-ounce soufflé ramekins with the 1 tablespoon butter. Set aside.

4. In a medium saucepan, melt the ¾ cup butter over medium heat. Add the brown sugar and, stirring continuously to dissolve the

sugar, bring the mixture to a simmer. Simmer, stirring frequently (the mixture will become bubbly and airy), until the mixture first lightens and then darkens slightly in color, about 5 minutes. Remove from the heat and let the mixture cool slightly, for about 5 minutes, but do not let the caramel harden (see Chef's Note page 102).

5. Divide the caramel sauce among the 8 ramekins. Lay a peach half, pitted-side down, onto the caramel in each ramekin. Set aside at room temperature while making the cake batter.

6. In a large mixing bowl, whisk together the cake flour, baking powder, salt, and the 1 cup remaining granulated sugar.

[recipe continues]

7. Place the 1 cup melted butter, the vanilla and almond extracts, and ⅓ cup of the cream in the bowl of a stand mixer fitted with the paddle attachment. Mix on low until just blended, about 1 minute. Add about half of the dry ingredients and turn on low just to blend, about 30 seconds. Add the rest of the dry ingredients and blend for another 30 seconds until no dry ingredients are showing through. Turn up the speed to medium and mix for about 5 minutes, stopping a couple of times to scrape down the sides of the bowl, until the mixture is light and fluffy and has the consistency of stiff icing.

8. Combine the egg yolks with the remaining ⅓ cup cream and add to the batter. Mix on medium speed for about 2 minutes, or until the batter is smooth and stiff, stopping to scrape down the sides of the bowl once or twice.

9. With a 1-cup measuring cup, scoop out a little less than a cup of batter and spoon onto the peach and caramel in each ramekin. Flatten the top of the batter with a spoon or spatula.

10. Place the filled ramekins directly on the oven rack with a baking sheet on the rack beneath to catch any caramel or batter that overflows. Bake until the tops are golden brown and firm to the touch and the caramel has started to bubble up around the edges, about 35 minutes.

11. Place the ramekins on a wire rack to cool slightly until the ramekins are just warm to the touch, about 5 minutes.

12. Run a knife around the inside edges of each ramekin to loosen the cake and invert onto a dessert plate. Spoon about 2 tablespoons of the raspberry sauce alongside each cake and serve.

| Chef's Note |

caramel sauce

If the caramel hardens before you have a chance to pour it into the ramekins, you can return the pan to low heat, add a little water, and heat, stirring often, until the syrup liquefies.

plum and ginger sorbet with cardamom cookies

You're looking for two qualities in the chilled base for fruit sorbets: a balance between sweet and tart, and a consistency that will create a smooth texture. When tasting the base before chilling, know that it should be slightly sweeter than what you want in the end product, as freezing will dull the sweetness slightly. The consistency of the base should be thick enough that if you spoon a small amount on a plate, it will not spread. Unless you have or are willing to buy a professional ice cream/sorbet maker, know that the texture of the ice cream from a commercially available ice cream maker will always be a little more granular than store-bought ice cream.

plum and ginger sorbet

There are fewer better ways to capture the essence of summer fruit than in a refreshing sorbet. Cook the fruit in the morning, allow it to cool, and let the ice cream maker do the rest. Once you get the hang of it (it's much easier than you can imagine), you can play with all the fruits of the summer and accents of complementary flavors. I chart the course of summer by watching the progression of old-world, heirloom-variety plums through the farmers' markets and find that deeply colored, gemlike varieties, such as Durantes and Elephant Hearts, make the deepest crimson, most flavorful sorbet.

MAKES 1 QUART; SERVES 5

2 **pounds** ripe, sweet plums, washed, pitted and quartered

2 **cups** cold water

1 **cup** sugar

One 1-inch piece fresh ginger, peeled

1 **tablespoon** lemon-flavored vodka or limoncello, or plain vodka

Pinch of kosher salt

1 **teaspoon** fresh lemon juice

16 Cardamom Cookies, for serving (page 104)

1. Place the ice cream maker core in the freezer 24 hours in advance.

2. In a medium stainless-steel saucepan, combine the plums, water, sugar, and ginger. Bring to a boil over medium-high heat, lower the heat, and simmer gently for 20 minutes. The plums should be very soft. Remove the ginger.

3. Transfer the mixture to a blender and process until very smooth. Whenever puréeing a hot mixture in a blender, remove the cap in the middle of the lid and place a thick towel over the hole while blending. Strain the fruit mixture through a medium-mesh sieve into a medium bowl, pushing the liquid through the solids. Stir in the vodka, salt, and lemon juice. Chill completely, at least 2 hours.

4. Place the chilled base in the ice cream machine and process according to the manufacturer's directions.

5. Serve a heaping ¾ cup of the sorbet with 2 cardamom cookies.

Wine Pairing

No one says you can't enjoy a little glass of Black Muscat even though you're just having a simple dessert. Try the sorbet with a generous splash over the top for a fun, slushy treat.

cardamom cookies

Cookies and sorbet are a light and refreshing way to draw a late-summer dinner to a close. The cardamom in these cookies acts as a perfect complement to the ginger in the Plum and Ginger Sorbet.

MAKES 3 DOZEN TWO-INCH COOKIES

1½ **cups** butter, softened (see Chef's Notes)

¾ **cup** sugar

2 **teaspoons** grated orange zest

2½ **cups** all-purpose flour

1½ **teaspoons** ground cardamom

½ **teaspoon** salt

1. In the bowl of a stand mixer fitted with the paddle attachment, cream the butter and sugar on medium speed until well blended, 2 to 3 minutes. Stop the mixer.

2. Add the zest, flour, cardamom, and salt to the butter mixture. Turn the mixer on low speed and blend until the dough comes together in a ball, about 2 minutes. Do not overmix.

3. Shape the dough into a disk, wrap in plastic, and chill for at least an hour (see Chef's Notes).

4. Preheat the oven to 350°F.

5. Line a baking sheet with a silcone mat or parchment paper.

6. On a lightly floured surface, roll the dough to a thickness of about ⅜ inch. Use a 2-inch cookie cutter to cut circles of dough.

7. Place the cookies on baking sheets with about ½ inch between the cookies.

8. Bake on the center rack of the oven until the cookies are lightly brown, 12 to 15 minutes. Let the cookies cool completely before removing from the pan.

Wine Pairing

Find a not-too-sweet Moscato for its hint of orange flavor to sip with this simple cookie.

| Chef's Notes |

why does the butter need to be softened?
The combining of sugar and butter in Step 1 is called "creaming." Soft butter combines with the sugar to create air in the batter. It is this air that will create leavening in the cookie.

why does cookie dough need to chill?
Chilling cookie dough helps the cookie to "set" once it starts baking, keeping it from spreading too much.

the new american cheese course

In every part of the country, a renaissance of artisan cheesemaking is taking place, and the pairing of cheese, fruit, and wine is taking on regional and contemporary twists. With blackberry bushes down the road and cherries at farm stands, these recipes are meant for dessert, with the last sips of wine from a late-summer meal.

For the Macerated Cherries on Goat Cheese Crostini, you will only need a small amount of the macerated cherries to top the crostini, but three cups is about the amount of cherries that come in a farm-stand basket, and they're lovely over vanilla ice cream, as well as other cheeses. Note that the cherries must be macerated for 24 hours.

"Behind every cheese," he muses, "there is a pasture of a different green under a different sky: meadows caked with salt that the tides of Normandy deposit every evening; meadows scented with aromas in the windy sunlight of Provence; there are different flocks, with their stablings and their transhumances; there are secret processes handed down over the centuries." *From Mr. Palomar by Italo Calvino*

fresh ricotta with blackberries and lime

When you have a little racy Barbera left over, try it with this cheese course, which will bring out the blackberry flavors in the wine.

SERVES 4

---

3 cups ripe fresh blackberries

2 to 3 tablespoons sugar, depending upon the sweetness of the blackberries

Zest of 1 lime, finely grated

Juice of 1 lime

8 ounces fresh whole-milk ricotta

---

1. Place 1½ cups of the blackberries in a blender and purée with the sugar. Strain the mixture through a fine-mesh sieve into a small bowl. Add half of the zest and the lime juice, stir, and refrigerate for at least 20 minutes.

2. Reserve the remaining blackberries and lime zest in the refrigerator.

3. Using a small 1-ounce ice-cream scoop, place 2 tablespoons of the ricotta in the middle of each of 4 small dessert plates. Toss the blackberry sauce with the remaining whole blackberries and spoon a quarter of the sauce around the outside of the ricotta on each plate. Garnish the ricotta with 1 or 2 blackberries and sprinkle the remaining zest over the ricotta and blackberries. Serve immediately.

humboldt fog cheese with fresh apricot conserve and crostini

Humboldt Fog is a lightly aged goat cheese with a thin ash layer that gives the cheese a distinctive and gently forest flavor. Try this cheese course with the last of your Viognier from dinner.

SERVES 8

6 fresh apricots (about 12 ounces), pitted and quartered

½ cup Chardonnay

¼ to ⅓ cup sugar, depending upon the sweetness of the apricots

½ vanilla bean, split open

1 baguette, cut into sixteen ¼-inch slices

¼ cup extra-virgin olive oil, or as needed, for brushing

12-ounce wedge Humboldt Fog cheese, cut into 8 thin slices

2 cups small, spring greens, such as mizuna or arugula

1. Preheat the oven to 350°F.

2. Place the apricots, Chardonnay, and sugar in a medium saucepan. Scrape the seeds from the vanilla bean into the pot. Bring to a simmer over medium heat. Simmer, stirring occasionally to keep the apricots from sticking, until most of the liquid has been cooked away and the mixture is soft and jam-like, 15 to 20 minutes. Reserve until needed.

3. Brush the baguette slices with olive oil and toast in the oven until just crispy and golden, 5 to 8 minutes.

4. Place a slice of cheese on each of 8 small plates. Place 2 tablespoons of the apricot conserve onto each of the baguette slices. Arrange 2 of the apricot crostini near the cheese and garnish with about ¼ cup of the greens.

macerated cherries on goat cheese crostini

So delicious with Pinot Noir, you may need to open another bottle!

SERVES 8

3 cups halved and pitted cherries

3 tablespoons Kirschwasser

1 tablespoon red wine vinegar

2 teaspoons sugar

1 baguette, cut into sixteen ¼-inch slices

¼ cup extra-virgin olive oil, or as needed for brushing

½ teaspoon sea salt

Two 6-ounce logs young goat cheese, each log cut into eight ¼-inch-thick rounds

1. Place the cherries in a bowl. Sprinkle the Kirschwasser and vinegar over the cherries and toss gently to coat. Sprinkle with sugar and toss again. Cover and refrigerate for 24 hours.

2. Drain the cherries from the liquid and place the cherries back in the refrigerator until needed. Place the liquid in a small saucepan, bring to a simmer over medium heat, and reduce until syrup-like, about 4 minutes. Remove from the heat and chill.

3. Just before you're ready to serve, preheat the oven to 350°F.

4. Brush the baguette slices with olive oil and sprinkle with a small amount of sea salt. Place the baguette slices on a baking sheet and toast in the oven until the bread is just golden, 5 to 8 minutes.

5. Remove from the oven and top each baguette round with a slice of goat cheese. Place two baguette slices on each of 8 small dessert plates. Toss the cherries with the syrup and place a couple of cherries on top of the goat cheese. Serve immediately.

harvest

The shifting of seasons in wine country is a subtle affair in autumn—the light growing amber and diffuse, vineyards glowing in the lowering, late-afternoon sun. The bright colors of berries and basil are replaced by a burnished palate of pears, apples, squash, and pumpkin. Olive trees, in their silvery shimmer, give up their plump, heavy harvest, and, in November, deep orange orbs of persimmons hang from otherwise bare branches. As night takes on an equal measure to day, wood smoke floats through lilac-tinged skies at twilight. The suspended, pale-sky days of summer slowly settle back to the earth and bring a yearned-for release from the long growing season. A sweet and yeasty smell can be caught in the air as crushed grape skins, given back to the vineyards, ferment in the gentle warmth of the waning sun.

The harvest urge to gather reaches a frenzied pace, then slips into cooler moods. For those who love to cook, coming inside to roast and bake and sip deeply colored wines offers repose in the shortening and finally cooling days. The flavors of fall are brought home, cooked down, and concentrated. Crisp, local apples play against reduced apple cider in Gravenstein Apple Salad with Mixed Salad Greens, Spiced Walnuts, Mustard Vinaigrette, Apple Gastrique, and Vella Cheddar Tuiles (page 122). Beet juice is simmered and condensed in Roasted Beet, Herbed Goat Cheese, and Hazelnut Timbales (page 115). Red wine becomes jamlike as it cooks slowly in Hanger Steak in Pinot Noir Sauce with Crispy Shallots and Point Reyes Blue Cheese (page 149).

And when the quick sear of the grill gives way to the slower, steady heat of the stove, warming spices begin to appear in soups such as Cauliflower Soup with Curried Fuji Apple (page 126) and Roasted Butternut Squash Soup with Toasted Pumpkin Seeds (page 129). As both the year and a meal come to a close, autumn's more bittersweet tones, those of persimmons and walnuts found at the season's last farmers' market, can be found in Persimmon Pudding Cake (page 157) and Walnut Tart with Maple Ice Cream (page 158).

panko-crusted fried oysters

Every Christmas Eve day, we head off to the coast to pick up oysters from the farms on Tomales Bay. On our way home, we drop off a couple of dozen oysters to friends along the way. There is usually a glass of wine or sparkling wine to greet our gift and another year of this West Coast tradition.

SERVES 6

---

24 small or small-medium oysters, shucked (about 2 cups of shucked oysters, depending on size)

1 cup all-purpose flour

1 teaspoon salt

½ teaspoon freshly ground black pepper

⅛ teaspoon cayenne pepper (optional)

2 large eggs

1 cup milk

1½ cups panko

3 cups vegetable oil, for frying, or as needed

½ cup Champagne-Mustard Sauce (recipe follows)

---

1. Drain the oysters well and pat dry.

2. Set up a breading assembly line. Sift the flour, salt, pepper, and cayenne (if using) together into a shallow dish. In a small bowl, lightly whip together the eggs and milk. Place the panko on a plate. Place a wire rack (or two smaller racks) on a baking sheet.

3. First dip the oysters in the flour, shaking off any excess, then the egg mixture, and then the panko, once again shaking off any excess. Place the oysters on the prepared racks and refrigerate for at least 30 minutes.

4. In a 3-quart saucepan over medium-high heat, heat 3 inches of vegetable oil to 365°F. Add the oysters to the pan in batches so as not to crowd the pan. Fry each batch, turning the oysters with tongs, until golden brown, 4 to 6 minutes. Drain the oysters on a paper towel–lined plate. Serve immediately with the Champagne-Mustard Sauce.

champagne-mustard sauce

MAKES ABOUT ½ CUP

---

4 tablespoons cold unsalted butter

2 tablespoons finely minced shallots

½ cup sparkling wine

¼ cup heavy cream

2 teaspoons Dijon mustard

Squeeze of fresh lemon

¼ teaspoon kosher salt

Freshly ground black pepper

---

1. In a small sauté pan, melt 2 tablespoons of the butter over medium heat. Add the shallots and sweat until translucent, about 2 minutes. Add the sparkling wine and adjust the heat so that the wine is simmering. Reduce the wine by half, about 4 minutes.

2. Add the cream and mustard and stir to blend. Remove the sauce from the heat and stir in the remaining 2 tablespoons of butter. Season with a squeeze of lemon and the salt and pepper.

salmon tartare with potato croquettes
Temptations, little bites of food meant to be shared around the table, have led the menu at Greystone's restaurant for over a decade.

SERVES 6 TO 8

salmon tartare

4 ounces smoked salmon fillet, minced very fine

1 tablespoon minced shallots

½ teaspoon lemon zest

¼ teaspoon Dijon mustard

1 teaspoon capers, rinsed and finely chopped

1 tablespoon chopped chives

2 tablespoons extra-virgin olive oil

¼ teaspoon salt

Pinch freshly ground black pepper

½ teaspoon fresh lemon juice, or as needed

potato croquettes

2 Idaho potatoes

1 large egg yolk

1 tablespoon crème fraîche or sour cream

2 teaspoons unsalted butter, melted

½ teaspoon kosher salt, or as needed

Pinch of ground white pepper

6 tablespoons all-purpose flour

1 whole egg, beaten

6 tablespoons panko

lemon crème fraîche

2 tablespoons crème fraîche or sour cream

½ teaspoon lemon juice

24 chervil or parsley sprigs or 1-inch-long chives

1. For the tartare: Mix all of the ingredients except the lemon juice and season with salt and pepper. Reserve in the refrigerator until just before serving. This can be prepared up to 8 hours in advance. Add the lemon juice to taste just before serving, otherwise it will begin to "cook" the salmon like a ceviche.

2. For the croquettes: Preheat the oven to 350°F. Bake the potatoes until tender, 45 to 60 minutes. Do not turn off the oven. Slice the potatoes in half lengthwise and, using a hot mitt and large spoon, remove the potato flesh from the skin while still warm. Discard the skins.

3. Run the potato flesh through a food mill or potato ricer into a large bowl.

4. Thoroughly mix in the egg yolk, créme fraîche, and butter. Season with the salt and pepper.

5. When completely cooled, use a small scoop or your hand to make 1-inch balls of the potato dough. Make a small indentation on the top with your thumb.

6. First dip the balls in the flour, shaking off any excess, then the egg and then the panko, once again shaking off any excess. Place the balls on a baking sheet lined with waxed paper, cover loosely and chill at least 1 hour. The recipe can be prepared up to here up to 24 hours before cooking.

7. Bake the balls in the 350°F oven until golden and crisp, about 18 minutes.

8. For the lemon crème fraîche: Mix the crème fraîche with the lemon juice.

9. Serve the croquettes with a tiny dollop of salmon tartare in the indentation, topped with the lemon crème fraîche and a sprig of chervil.

roasted beet, herbed goat cheese, and hazelnut timbales

This is a very uptown signature dish of David Thater, chef extraordinaire for Greystone's Special Events department. Chef Thater uses custom-cut molds, but here we use standard stainless-steel molds that are 3 inches wide by 1¾ inches high. (Note that you'll need to start the recipe at least a day in advance.)

The combination of sweet beets, tart and creamy goat cheese, and the forest-flavored crunch of hazelnuts is a Northern California classic that David took up a notch or two to create a this dazzling first-course dish. The elegant presentation and gemlike glitter of the red and golden beets has become a signature starter for evening events that are meant to impress. Although the recipe takes some time, everything can be done in advance, leaving only the unmolding of the timbales for the end.

SERVES 4

---

1 **pound** red beets, tops removed

1 **pound** golden beets, tops removed

2 **tablespoons** olive oil

2 bay leaves

5 **teaspoons** kosher salt

16 peppercorns

3 **tablespoons** red balsamic vinegar

3 **tablespoons** golden balsamic vinegar

4 **ounces** soft, fresh goat cheese (preferably Laura Chenel)

1 **tablespoon** finely chopped fresh flat-leaf parsley

1 **tablespoon** finely chopped fresh chives

1 **teaspoon** fresh thyme leaves

2 endives, separated into individual leaves

1 **cup** mâche or arugula leaves

¼ **cup** coarsely ground skinned hazelnuts

2 **teaspoons** fruity olive oil, or as needed to garnish

1 **teaspoon** fleur de sel, or as needed to garnish

½ **teaspoon** coarsely ground black pepper, or as needed to garnish

---

1. Preheat the oven to 325°F.

2. Place the beets in two separate shallow roasting dishes. Add enough water to come three-quarters of the way up the beets. Add a tablespoon of the olive oil, a bay leaf, about ½ teaspoon of salt, and 8 peppercorns to each dish. Mix well.

3. Cover with aluminum foil and place in the oven. Bake until a skewer inserted into the center of the beets goes through easily, 45 to 60 minutes, depending on the size of the beets. Check the water level from time to time and add more water, 1 cup at a time, as necessary. (Do not let the beets go dry.)

4. Remove the beets from the oven, drain, and cool. When cool enough to handle, peel and separately shred each set of beets with a box grater.

5. Toss the red beets with the red balsamic vinegar and 2 teaspoons of salt. Toss the golden beets with the golden balsamic vinegar and 2 teaspoons of salt.

6. Over two medium bowls, place the shredded beets in separate fine-mesh sieves. Place a plate on top of the beets and a weight on top of the plate to press liquid from them. Cover and refrigerate overnight.

[recipe continues]

7. Bring the goat cheese to room temperature. Mix in the parsley, chives, and thyme and reserve until needed.

8. Place four 2-by-2½-inch or four 3-by-1¾-inch stainless-steel cylinders on a small baking sheet (or something else flat that will fit in the refrigerator).

9. Reserve the accumulated juice from the red beets and discard the yellow beet juice. Spoon one-quarter of the pressed red beets into each form. Tap down firmly with a glass spice jar wrapped in plastic, making sure that the surface is flat. Add one-quarter of the golden beets on top of the red beets and tap down firmly. Put one-quarter of the herbed goat cheese on top of golden beets to fill the form. Flatten with a butter knife. Place in the refrigerator for at least 2 hours to allow the timbales to "set up."

10. In a small saucepan over medium heat, simmer the reserved red beet juice until it is reduced to a sauce-like consistency, about 5 minutes (the sauce will thicken a little more when refrigerated). Reserve in the refrigerator until needed.

11. When ready to serve, remove the timbales from the molds by running a warm, wet knife around the inside rim to release the goat cheese from the sides of the mold. Push the timbales from the bottom with one hand, inverting it onto your other hand. Place each timbale, goat cheese side up, onto a salad plate. Lay 3 endive leaves around each timbale. Nestle a handful of mâche or arugula against the timbale. Sprinkle 1 tablespoon of hazelnuts on top of the goat cheese. Drizzle 1 teaspoon of the reduced beet juice (or gastrique; see Chef's Note) over the plate. Drizzle ½ teaspoon of fruity olive oil over the greens and season with ¼ teaspoon of fleur de sel and freshly ground black pepper. Serve immediately.

Wine Pairing

Serve a light Pinot Noir or even a Pinot Noir rosé with this salad course.

| Chef's Note |

gastriques

A gastrique is a type of reduction that typically combines something sweet (such as sugar or fruit juices) and an acid such as vinegar or citrus juice. It is often used in savory dishes that include fruit. The gastrique will firm up further as it cools, so don't over-reduce.

wilted greens with hazelnut oil, eggs, and fennel on toast

Noted chef and cookbook author John Ash is the executive chef for CIA's Sophisticated Palate program for culinary enthusiasts. This recipe is his favorite variation on the eggs Benedict theme, and showcases the unique flavor of sourdough bread, a San Francisco specialty. The hazelnut oil gives the "meaty" flavor of Canadian bacon that is traditionally used. The end result is lighter and brighter than the heavy hollandaise sauce original. You can substitute any other nut oils that you like. This recipe is quick to prepare and perfect for brunch, lunch, or supper.

SERVES 4

---

4 large eggs, preferably free-range

1 large fennel bulb (about 1 pound), trimmed

4 tablespoons toasted hazelnut oil

2 teaspoons salt, or as needed

½ teaspoon freshly ground black pepper, or as needed

1 quart lightly packed watercress leaves (about 2 bunches)

1 quart lightly packed young spinach leaves

1 to 2 tablespoons fresh lemon juice

4 thick slices sourdough bread, lightly toasted

¼ cup freshly grated pecorino or Parmesan cheese

---

1. Place the eggs in a small saucepan with cold water to cover by at least ½ inch. Bring to a boil, reduce the heat, and simmer gently for 1½ minutes. Drain and cool the eggs under running water. Peel and reserve in the refrigerator. The whites should be set but yolks will still be runny when you cut into them.

2. Trim the fennel of any dark spots, then cut in half and remove the core and woody base. With a mandoline or very sharp knife, shave the fennel lengthwise into ⅟₁₆-inch-thick slices. Warm 2 tablespoons of the oil in a large sauté pan over medium-high heat. Add the fennel and sauté until just tender, about 4 minutes. Season with salt and pepper and reserve warm.

3. Add the watercress and spinach to a large bowl and toss with the remaining 2 tablespoons of oil. Heat the sauté pan again over medium-high heat and sauté the greens until they just begin to wilt, about 1 minute. Season with salt and pepper and a drizzle of lemon juice.

4. Place the toast on 4 plates and top each with one-quarter of the warm greens. Divide the fennel among the toasts and place 1 egg on top of each of the toasts. Sprinkle 1 tablespoon of cheese over each egg and serve immediately. As guests cut into the eggs, the yolks will run and combine with the rest of the ingredients, making a delicious sauce.

Wine Pairing

A lightly oaked Chardonnay will pick up the nutty tones without overpowering the other salad flavors.

| Chef's Note |

Once better known for its walnut trees than for its vineyards, Napa Valley is now producing nut oils that rival those of France. Nut oils provide a sweet, roasted, fragrant addition to dishes with cold-weather ingredients. High-quality nut oils can be expensive and go rancid more quickly than other oils. Buy in small quantities and keep tightly covered in the refrigerator. Once refrigerated, bring to room temperature before using.

gravenstein apple salad with mixed salad greens, spiced walnuts, mustard vinaigrette, apple gastrique, and vella cheddar tuiles

A Northern California riff on one of fall's favorite couplings—apple pie and Cheddar cheese—was the initial inspiration for Chef Polly Lapettito to come up with this sweet, salty, and spicy salad. The very-simple-to-make tuiles are a delicate take on the same cheese that oozes from a grilled cheese sandwich and then crisps on the hot skillet.

Gravenstein apples are an heirloom variety that come from mostly heritage orchards in nearby Sonoma County. An early and local favorite, they have an appealing balance of sweet and tart and are good eating either raw or cooked.

SERVES 6

---

apple gastrique

1½ **cups** unfiltered apple cider

½ **cup** apple cider vinegar

mustard vinaigrette

1 **tablespoon** finely minced shallot

¼ **cup** apple cider vinegar

½ **teaspoon** Colman's dry mustard

½ **teaspoon** honey

2 **tablespoons** walnut oil

½ **cup** olive oil

½ **teaspoon** salt, or as needed

⅛ **teaspoon** finely ground pepper, or as needed

salad

3 crisp Gravenstein apples
(or substitute Braeburn, Pink Lady, or Fuji)

5½ **ounces** spring salad greens

1 celery stalk, trimmed, and cut into thin slices on the diagonal

18 Spiced Walnuts, cut in half (page 124)

6 Vella Cheddar Tuiles (page 124)

---

1. For the gastrique: In a medium, nonreactive saucepan over medium-high heat, bring the apple cider and cider vinegar to a boil. Reduce the heat until the mixture reaches a gentle simmer and reduce the liquid until thick and syrupy, 20 to 25 minutes.

2. For the vinaigrette: Place the shallot and cider vinegar in a medium bowl and allow to macerate for 30 minutes.

3. Add the dry mustard and honey and whisk to blend. Slowly add the walnut oil and whisk to emulsify. Slowly add the olive oil and whisk to emulsify. Taste and season with salt and pepper.

4. For the salad: Just before serving, halve and core the apples. Cut each half into very thin slices on a mandoline (or with a sharp knife). Place the apple slices in a large mixing bowl and toss immediately with about 2 tablespoons of the vinaigrette to coat.

5. Add the greens, celery, and walnuts. Toss gently. Starting with 2 tablespoons of the vinaigrette, pour the dressing around the bowl's rim and toss. Add more vinaigrette as desired and toss.

6. Divide the salad among 6 chilled salad plates. Drizzle about 2 teaspoons of gastrique around the rim of each plate. Place a tuile on top of the salad and serve.

Wine Pairing

Find a young, dry Pinot Blanc to meet the demands of this complex salad. The acid in the wine will keep your palate refreshed for more.

spiced walnuts

Use the extra walnuts to sprinkle onto grain dishes or to eat as a snack.

MAKES ABOUT 2 CUPS

---

2 cups walnut halves

2 tablespoons olive oil

1 teaspoon salt

1 tablespoon sugar

⅛ teaspoon ground black pepper

⅛ teaspoon ground cinnamon

⅛ teaspoon ground allspice

⅛ teaspoon cayenne pepper

---

1. Preheat the oven to 350°F.

2. Toss the walnut halves with the olive oil to coat. Toss with the remaining ingredients.

3. Place the walnuts on a baking sheet in an even layer and roast until toasted, shaking the pan frequently, about 10 minutes. Remove the walnuts from the oven and place on a plate to cool.

vella cheddar tuiles

Vella cheese is made in small batches from the milk of cows that graze in the verdant pasturelands of Sonoma County. Extra tuiles can be eaten with soup or other salads.

MAKES ABOUT TWELVE 2½-INCH TUILES

5½ ounces grated Vella Cheddar (about 1½ cups)

1 teaspoon all-purpose flour

½ teaspoon fresh thyme leaves

Pinch of cayenne pepper

---

1. Preheat the oven to 400°F.

2. Toss together the cheese, flour, thyme leaves, and cayenne to combine.

3. Line a baking sheet with a silicone mat. Place a heaping tablespoon of the cheese mixture in a small mound on the silicone mat. Pat the mound flat. Repeat with the remaining cheese mixture, leaving about an inch around each tuile.

4. Place the baking sheet in the oven and bake until golden brown, 8 to 10 minutes (do not burn). Remove the pan from the oven and place on a wire rack to cool.

5. Using a spatula, gently remove the tuiles from the silicone mat and store, covered in an airtight container, at room temperature.

mixed field greens, shaved fennel, red onion, and pear in sherry vinaigrette

Catherine Brandel was a founding member of the Greystone faculty and one of Northern California's most beloved chefs. Her generosity of both spirit and cooking laid one of Greystone's most enduring foundations.

Shaved vegetable salads were one of Catherine's favorite concoctions, and the mandoline was one of her most-used kitchen tools. This salad's mellow vinaigrette acts as a foil to the crisp sweetness of the paper-thin fennel and pear.

SERVES 4

---

2 shallots (about 2 ounces), peeled and cut in half

2 garlic cloves, peeled

1 small bay leaf

⅛ **teaspoon** mustard seeds

¼ **teaspoon** coarse sea salt, or as needed

Freshly ground black pepper, as needed

½ **teaspoon** fresh thyme leaves

2 **teaspoons plus 6 tablespoons** extra-virgin olive oil

1 fennel bulb

½ small red onion (about 3 ounces), peeled

2 **tablespoons** sherry vinegar

3 **ounces** mixed greens, washed and dried

1 ripened pear (French Butter, Anjou, or Bosc)

---

1. Preheat the oven to 350°F.

2. On a 6-inch square of aluminum foil, place the shallots, garlic, bay leaf, mustard seeds, ¼ teaspoon sea salt, pepper to taste, thyme, and the 2 teaspoons olive oil. Fold the foil over the ingredients and place in the oven. Roast until the garlic and shallots are tender and slightly caramelized, about 1 hour. Remove from the oven, open the foil, and let cool to room temperature.

3. Trim the fennel of any dark spots, then cut in half and remove the core and woody base. With a mandoline or very sharp knife, shave the fennel lengthwise into ¹⁄₁₆-inch-thick slices. Place in a small bowl, cover with a damp towel, and refrigerate until ready to use.

4. Cut the onion into ¹⁄₁₆-inch-thick slices. Place the onion slices in a bowl and cover with ice water. Soak for at least 30 minutes, changing out the water once halfway through.

5. Place the cooled shallots and garlic in a blender with the vinegar and blend until smooth, about 20 seconds. Slowly add the 6 tablespoons olive oil and blend to emulsify. Place the vinaigrette in a bowl and season with salt and pepper.

6. Drain the onion and place in a large salad bowl with the fennel and greens. Starting with 2 tablespoons of vinaigrette, toss lightly to coat, adding more vinaigrette as necessary. Adjust the seasoning with salt and pepper. Just before serving, core the pear, cut into as thin slices as possible, and toss with the salad, separating the pear slices. Serve immediately.

Wine Pairing

Pinot Grigio is a fun way to echo the fresh fennel and pears in this dish.

cauliflower soup with curried fuji apple

This admittedly buttery soup is adapted from a recipe created by Todd Humphries, a CIA graduate who was the executive chef of the Wine Spectator restaurant at Greystone in the late 1990s and is now the chef and partner in St. Helena's Martini House.

The idea of this recipe comes from the combination of cauliflower and curry in Indian cuisine. With leeks and onions as background flavors, and white port smoothing out the flavors overall, the sweetness of the apple reminds you of the orchard and root vegetable days to come.

SERVES 6

---

6 tablespoons unsalted butter

2 tablespoons olive oil

2 leeks (about 8 ounces each), white and tender green parts only, split lengthwise, cut into ¼-inch slices, and cleaned and drained thoroughly

1 Spanish onion (about 8 to 10 ounces), peeled and cut into thin slices

1 parsnip (about 4 ounces), peeled, trimmed, and cut into thin slices

½ teaspoon kosher salt

1 head of cauliflower (about 2 pounds), trimmed, cored, and cut into thin slices

¼ cup white port or pale dry sherry

6 cups light chicken or vegetable stock

1 small bay leaf

Squeeze of fresh lemon juice

Pinch of cayenne pepper

1 teaspoon salt, or as needed

¼ teaspoon freshly ground white pepper, or as needed

1 Fuji apple (about 8 ounces), cored

½ teaspoon good-quality curry powder

---

1. In a heavy-bottomed soup pot over medium heat, melt 5 tablespoons of the butter with the olive oil. Add the leeks, onion, parsnip, and salt and sweat, covered, stirring occasionally, until the onion is translucent and the other vegetables have softened, about 8 minutes. Add the cauliflower and sweat, stirring often, until the cauliflower begins to soften, about 3 minutes longer.

2. Increase the heat to medium-high and add the port. Reduce the liquid until it is almost all gone, about 3 minutes.

3. Add the stock and bay leaf, bring to a simmer, and cook, uncovered, for 30 minutes.

4. Remove the bay leaf and drain the solids, reserving the liquids. Purée the solids with an immersion or stand blender using a small amount of the reserved liquid (about 1 cup). Reserve 1 cup of the purée and combine the rest with the remaining reserved liquid in a bowl, stirring well to blend.

5. Strain the soup through a fine-mesh sieve into a large pot. Add the reserved 1 cup purée, stir to blend, and warm the soup over medium heat. Season the soup with a squeeze of fresh lemon juice, a sprinkle of cayenne pepper, and salt and pepper.

6. While the soup is warming, core and cut the apple into a small dice. In a small sauté pan over medium heat, melt the remaining 1 tablespoon of butter, then add the apple and curry powder. Cook, stirring gently, until the apple has softened just a touch, about 2 minutes.

7. Divide the warm soup among 6 soup bowls. Sprinkle the diced apple over each bowl and serve immediately.

Wine Pairing

An off-dry Gewürztraminer complements the fun flavors of this soup.

using an immersion blender

Immersion blenders (also referred to as hand blenders) are one of those kitchen devices that have found their way from the professional kitchen into the home kitchen. Rather than lugging hot liquids from pot to blender or food processor and back again, using an immersion blender saves steps and eliminates the problems with puréeing hot liquids.

There are quite a few models and many bells and whistles that come with different immersion blenders. All are wand-shaped devices that have an enclosed blender blade on the bottom. When the bottom of the blender is fully immersed in liquid and turned on, it quickly and thoroughly creates smooth purées for foods such as soups and smoothies.

roasted butternut squash soup with toasted pumpkin seeds

Adapted from the restaurant at Greystone, this recipe shows how roasting vegetables intensifies their flavors. Toasted pumpkin seed oil has become more readily available, but you can substitute white truffle oil.

SERVES 6

---

1 butternut squash (2½ to 3 pounds)

3 tablespoons olive oil

1 cinnamon stick

1 star anise pod

¼ teaspoon aniseseed

One 1-inch piece fresh ginger, peeled and crushed

1 onion (8 to 10 ounces), peeled and thinly sliced

5 cups rich chicken or vegetable stock

½ cup heavy cream

1 teaspoon salt, or as needed

¼ teaspoon ground white pepper, or as needed

Pinch of cayenne pepper

2 teaspoons toasted pumpkin seed oil, for garnish

2 tablespoons Toasted Pumpkin Seeds (page 130), for garnish

---

1. Preheat the oven to 400°F.

2. Cut the butternut squash in half. Scrape out the seeds and surrounding fibers. Rub the cut surface of the squash with 1 tablespoon of the olive oil. Place the squash, cut-side down, on a parchment paper–lined baking sheet and place in the oven. Roast the squash until the squash collapses and the flesh is very tender, about 50 minutes. Remove from the oven and, when cool enough to handle, scrape the flesh from the skin and set aside.

3. Tie the cinnamon stick, star anise, aniseseed, and ginger in cheesecloth to make a sachet. In a large soup pot over medium-high heat, warm the remaining 2 tablespoons olive oil. Add the onion and sauté until translucent, 4 to 5 minutes. Add the chicken stock and sachet, bring to a boil, and reduce the heat and simmer, stirring occasionally, for 10 minutes. Add the reserved squash, stir, and simmer for 10 more minutes.

4. Remove the sachet from the soup and, with an immersion or stand blender, purée the soup until smooth. (Note: If using a stand blender, remove the plastic cap in the middle of the lid and place a thick towel over the lid while blending.)

5. Strain the soup through a fine-mesh sieve into a large saucepan and gently rewarm over medium-low heat. Add the cream and stir to blend. Season the soup with salt, pepper, and cayenne. If the soup is too thick, add a bit more stock or cream and bring the soup back to a simmer.

6. Divide the soup among 6 bowls. Garnish each bowl with a drizzle of pumpkin seed oil and a sprinkle of toasted pumpkin seeds. Serve immediately.

Wine Pairing

A Riesling with a touch of sweetness is a natural pairing for the spice in this satisfying soup.

toasted pumpkin seeds

Make a batch to have on hand as a snack or as a garnish for soup or salads. If you can't find pumpkin seeds, toasted sunflower seeds will do in a pinch.

MAKES ½ CUP

½ **cup** hulled pumpkin seeds

1 **tablespoon** extra-virgin olive oil

¼ **teaspoon** kosher salt, or as needed

Pinch of cayenne pepper, or as needed

Place the pumpkin seeds and oil in a small skillet over medium heat and toast, stirring often, until the seeds pop and turn crispy and brown, 5 to 6 minutes. Remove from heat, season well with salt and cayenne, and toss again. Pour onto a plate to cool. Store in an airtight container in the refrigerator.

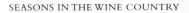

pumpkin and sage polenta

A steamy bowl of polenta, one of the world's great comfort foods, can keep the chill from any fall evening. Try to cook the polenta on as low a heat and as slowly as possible. Once the polenta is simmering, it is not necessary to stir all of the time, just often enough to keep it from sticking and scorching. This variation cozies up a trilogy of classic Italian fall flavors—musky sage, the caramelized sugars of roasted pumpkin, and cornmeal—into a homey side dish to accompany pork or poultry (see Roasted Pork Tenderloin with Apple and Bacon Compote, page 147)

SERVES 4 TO 6

---

5 cups chicken or vegetable stock

1 teaspoon kosher salt

½ teaspoon freshly ground white pepper

⅛ teaspoon freshly ground nutmeg (or a few grinds in a mill)

1 teaspoon rubbed dried sage

1 cup yellow coarsely ground polenta (stone-ground, if available)

½ cup pumpkin purée

½ cup grated fontina cheese

1 to 2 tablespoons unsalted butter

---

1. In a large pot over medium-high heat, bring the stock, salt, pepper, nutmeg, and sage to a boil. Add the polenta in a slow, gentle stream, whisking constantly. Reduce the heat to a very gentle simmer and continue whisking until polenta begins to thicken, about 5 minutes.

2. Using a wooden spoon, cook and stir the polenta from time to time until it is soft and creamy, about 20 minutes. If the polenta becomes too stiff, add a small amount of water. Add the pumpkin purée, cheese, and butter and stir to blend and melt the cheese and butter. Taste and adjust the seasoning as needed with salt and pepper. Serve immediately.

chilaquiles

Depending upon the variation, chilaquiles is a traditional Mexican soup/stew/casserole that is a staple street food. This version comes from Chef Bill Briwa, who often works with Hispanic foods and has been a chef-instructor at Greystone since 1995. Cooked and shredded chicken or turkey can be added for a whole-meal dish.

SERVES 6 TO 8

5 garlic cloves

¼ **cup** vegetable oil

1 bunch Swiss chard (about 1 pound), center rib removed, leaves cut into 1-inch ribbons, and rinsed well (about 8 loosely packed cups)

8 **ounces** mushrooms (a variety, if available), cleaned and cut into ¼-inch-thick slices

6 Roma tomatoes (about 2 pounds), cut in half and most of the seeds squeezed out

1 medium white onion (about 8 ounces), peeled and cut into 6 wedges, plus ¼ cup finely minced

6 pasillo chiles, cut in half, seeds removed, and softened in warm water

1 **quart** vegetable stock

1 to 2 **teaspoons** salt, or as needed

2 **teaspoons** sugar

8 **ounces** thick, no-salt tortilla chips

1 **cup** queso añejo, crumbled

⅓ **cup** sour cream

2 **tablespoons** whole milk

12 fresh cilantro leaves

1. Preheat the broiler to high.

2. Dry roast the garlic in a heavy skillet over medium heat, stirring often, until soft, about 15 minutes. When cool enough to handle, peel the garlic.

3. In a large sauté pan, warm 3 tablespoons of the vegetable oil over medium-high heat. Add the chard and mushrooms and cook, stirring often, until the chard is tender and the mushrooms are lightly browned, about 5 minutes. Reserve at room temperature until needed.

4. Place the tomatoes and onion wedges on a baking sheet and roast under the broiler until softened and beginning to blacken on the first side, about 5 minutes. Turn the tomatoes and onion and continue to broil until they start to blacken on other side, about 5 minutes.

5. Remove the tomatoes and onion from the oven and, when cool enough to handle, peel away the worst of the charred skins. Reserve the tomatoes and onion, along with any juices that have accumulated.

6. In a blender, combine the garlic, tomatoes and onion and their juices, chiles, and 2 cups of the stock and blend until a smooth purée is achieved, about 1 minute.

7. In a 12-inch cast-iron skillet, heat the remaining tablespoon of oil over medium-high heat. Add the tomato purée all at once, along with rest of stock, the salt, and sugar and stir to combine. Bring to a simmer and simmer until thick enough to coat the back of a spoon, about 8 to 10 minutes.

8. Add the chips, along with the reserved chard and mushrooms. Stir well to coat the chips with sauce and bring back to a simmer. Simmer until the chips have softened, about 4 to 5 minutes.

9. Divide the chilaquiles onto plates or wide bowls and sprinkle with the minced onion and queso añejo. In a small bowl, thin the sour cream with the milk and drizzle over the chilaquiles. Top with the cilantro leaves and serve.

Wine Pairing

A fuller bodied Blanc de Noirs sparkling wine turns this dish into a party.

Chef's Note

Both roasting under a broiler and dry-roasting ingredients on the stove top deepen the flavors of even the simplest of ingredients.

Queso añejo is a Mexican cheese that is rolled in paprika to enhance its sharp, salty flavor. Feta or Parmesan can be substituted, but see if you can find the *queso añejo*, which is more and more available.

Lesson in Wine:
pinot noir

As the grapes are picked and brought in and the vineyards become tawny colored, thoughts of wine turn from white to red. In between the heat and bright flavors of summer and the deep, darker tastes of winter, many of the earthy, forest-like essences of Pinot Noir begin to come into the kitchen.

---

an introduction to pinot noir

The latest news that Pinot Noir has more genes in its DNA than humans sums it up: Pinot Noir is an endlessly fascinating grape variety. Admired for centuries for its ethereal, supple, sensual character and for being an elusive grape to master, Pinot Noir is the true seductress of the wine world. Pinot Noir fruit tends to be low in tannins and high in acid, with flavors that include cherries, berries, mushrooms, dried leaves, and perhaps a touch of cocoa powder.

The most notable Pinot Noir growing and production region in the world is Burgundy, where chalky soils, the way in which a vineyard is situated, and a cool climate all contribute to its ultimate complexity. Also notable is the importance of Pinot Noir in producing

Champagne and other top-quality sparkling wines from around the world. Oregon, New Zealand, and, now, even Germany all produce top-notch Pinot Noir with modern grape-growing and winemaking sensibilities, accelerating the learning curve for vintners and drinkers alike and resulting in relatively fast successes for these regions. In California, where it has taken decades to establish the best locations and clones for Pinot Noir, we have several regions that produce wines of great distinction: Carneros, Russian River Valley, Anderson Valley, Santa Maria Valley, Arroyo Grande Valley, and Santa Lucia Highlands.

---

a few general styles

Simple, relatively inexpensive Pinot Noir should be clean and fruity, with bright acid. The color isn't saturated; rather, you should be able to read through the wine in a glass, if you try. Look for bright garnet wines and drink them young. A touch of cinnamon on the nose might indicate the use of a little oak, which is fine. In California, these wines can come from any of the mentioned regions, but also look for Central Coast or Sonoma Coast as indicators of good quality and good value.

Many California vintners aim to produce "Burgundian-style" wines with gentle oak treatment and enhanced earthy aromas and flavors. While never sparing the ripe sour cherry and rhubarb notes, there is an added layer of wild mushrooms, fresh earth, new leather, and sometimes the slightest bit of barnyard. This style of wine is elegant, layered, and tends to make you ramble on poetically. Throughout California, many vintners also practice some traditional techniques, mainly letting the wine "make itself" with minimal human intervention.

On the modern side, ripeness and full-on fruitiness is also executed with aplomb by many top producers in California. These are the cult Pinots, often unrestrained and wandering into sweet black and Bing cherry arenas with spicy new oak, higher alcohols, and sometimes almost Zinfandel-like characteristics. Though these may seem like an extreme variation of the grape, they are an authentic expression nonetheless. Core flavors and structure remain, but in a voluptuous, souped-up style that appeals to many.

what makes pinot noir a special wine

André Tchelistcheff declared that "God made Cabernet Sauvignon, whereas the devil made Pinot Noir." The grape is difficult to grow, for many technical reasons, requiring specific soil types and careful winemaking in order to produce wines of real distinction. The entire process is a labor of love that requires artistry on the part of the winemaker and a true appreciation on the part of the recipient.

a brief riff on foods that love pinot noir

Gamey flavors like duck, quail, squab, lamb. Anything with mushrooms and perhaps a little bacon. Coq au vin is lovely. A simple pork, veal, or beef roast with herbs will allow the wine to shine. Braises. Root vegetables. Soft-ripened cheeses. And truffles!

serving, storage, aging

Serve Pinot Noir a little cooler than you would a Cabernet Sauvignon—at about 55°F. Store as you would any other wine, on its side in a cool, slightly humid, and dark area. No vibrations. Good Pinot Noir will develop intriguing characteristics over 2 to 5 years, and great Pinot Noirs will age for longer, but if you want to retain some of the beguiling fruit, be careful after 10 years unless there is a track record for the wine.

steamed manila clams with romesco sauce

Trips to Tomales Bay, where nutrient-rich waters wash in from the Pacific tides, are the inspiration for this dish. Adapted from a favorite dish at Greystone's restaurant, the clams glisten with the garlicky and slightly spicy romesco sauce, creating a broth born to be sopped up with the sourdough bread. Other small clams such as cherrystones can be used.

SERVES 6 AS AN APPETIZER, 4 AS A MAIN COURSE

---

5 pounds manila clams

¼ cup butter

2 tablespoons minced garlic

2 tablespoons minced shallots

1½ cups white wine

1 bay leaf

1 tablespoon fresh thyme leaves

1½ cups Romesco Sauce (page 140)

Salt, as needed

Freshly ground black pepper, as needed

2 tablespoons extra-virgin olive oil

1 sourdough baguette, cut into 12 slices (or 8 if dish is being used as a main course)

¼ cup olive oil, for brushing

1 clove garlic, peeled and crushed

6 sprigs fresh flat-leaf parsley, or 2 tablespoons chopped parsley

---

1. Soak the clams in salted water for 1 to 2 hours. When ready to start cooking, drain the clams and rinse well. Preheat the grill or broiler for toasting bread.

2. In a large pot with a cover, melt the butter over medium heat. Add the garlic and shallots and sweat, covered, until just softened, about 1 minute. Add the clams, wine, bay leaf, and thyme and turn the heat to high. Cover and cook the clams, stirring the pan occasionally, until all of the clams open, 4 to 5 minutes. Remove the clams with tongs and place in warmed bowls, discarding any clams that do not open.

3. Add the romesco sauce to the pot with the wine and butter liquid, stir to combine, and bring to a simmer over medium-high heat. Reduce the heat and simmer gently for 4 minutes. Season with salt and pepper and finish with the extra-virgin olive oil.

4. While the sauce is simmering, brush the bread with the olive oil. Grill or broil until lightly browned. Rub with the garlic clove.

5. Divide the sauce over the clams and sprinkle with fresh parsley. Serve immediately with 2 slices of toasted bread per person.

romesco sauce

Romesco sauce can also be used on sandwiches or served as a sauce over pasta. If fresh tomatoes are not in season, use 3 cups good-quality canned tomatoes.

MAKES ABOUT 3 CUPS

---

1 large or **2** small ancho chiles (about ½ ounce)

⅔ cup olive oil, or as needed

2 slices artisan bread, cut into large dice

3 large, ripe heirloom tomatoes (1 pound each), peeled, cored, seeded, and coarsely chopped

3 garlic cloves, peeled

1 red bell pepper (about 6 ounces), roasted, peeled, and seeded

½ cup almonds, lightly toasted

½ cup hazelnuts, toasted and skins removed

1 tablespoon pimentón (Spanish paprika)

3 tablespoons sherry vinegar, or as needed to adjust acidity

1 teaspoon salt, or as needed

¼ teaspoon freshly ground black pepper, or as needed

---

1. Remove the seeds from the ancho chiles and soak the chiles in warm water until well softened, about 1 hour.

2. In a medium sauté pan over medium heat, warm 2 tablespoons of the olive oil. Add the bread pieces and sauté, stirring and turning the slices frequently, until golden brown and toasted, about 4 minutes. Remove from the heat.

3. Purée all of the ingredients except the remaining olive oil in a blender. Drizzle in the olive oil and blend to emulsify. The final sauce should be slightly chunky, with the nuts retaining some of their texture.

4. Adjust the seasoning if necessary and, if not acidic enough, add more sherry vinegar as desired.

Wine Pairing

A Rhône-style Grenache rosé will stand up to the spiced and roasted flavors of the romesco.

| Chef's Note |

The romesco sauce can be made well in advance (about 2 days), making this an easy-to-assemble dish for a gathering. This recipe yields enough to make the Steamed Clams recipe twice. It freezes well and can be stored for up to a month.

mushroom, winter squash, and red wine panade

Another of Catherine Brandel's (see page 125) earthy and elemental dishes, this is a variation of a panade recipe that Catherine brought with her from Chez Panisse. A traditional panade is made with bread crumbs, but using whole slices of a dense, country-style bread, along with the mushrooms and squash, creates a real meatiness in this non-meat-based dish. For vegetarians, vegetable stock can easily replace the chicken stock.

SERVES 6

½ **cup** olive oil

4 onions (about 2 pounds), peeled and cut into ⅛-inch slices

5 garlic cloves, peeled and cut into ⅛-inch slices

1 bay leaf

6 fresh thyme sprigs

10 slices country-style, sourdough bread (each about ½ inch thick)

1 cup red wine

1 pound mushrooms (cremini, or combination of wild mushrooms, such as chanterelles), cleaned and cut into ¼-inch-thick slices

½ **teaspoon** salt

¼ **teaspoon** freshly ground black pepper

6 cups chicken or vegetable stock

2 pounds butternut squash, peeled and cut into ½-inch disks

½ **cup** freshly grated Asiago cheese

½ **cup** freshly grated Parmigiano-Reggiano cheese

1. Preheat the oven to 350°F.

2. In a large and deep sauté pan, warm ¼ cup of the olive oil over medium heat. Add the onions, stir to coat, and cover. Cook, stirring often until golden brown, about 10 minutes. Remove the cover, add the garlic, bay leaf, and thyme, and continue to cook, stirring occasionally, until the onions are very tender and slightly caramelized, about 25 minutes.

3. While the onions are cooking, place the bread slices on a baking pan and toast in the oven for a couple of minutes, or just until golden. Remove from the oven. Brush both sides of the bread slices with 2 tablespoons of the oil and reserve. Raise the oven temperature to 400°F.

4. Once the onions have caramelized, turn the heat to medium-high and add the red wine. Scrape the bottom of the pan to release any caramelized onion bits and reduce the wine by half, about 10 minutes.

5. In a medium sauté pan, while the wine is reducing, warm the last 2 tablespoons olive oil over medium-high heat. Add the mushrooms and cook, stirring, until the mushrooms are just tender and lightly browned, about 5 minutes. Season the mushrooms with salt and pepper and reserve at room temperature.

6. Once the wine is reduced, add the chicken stock to the onion mixture. Add the mushrooms and simmer for 30 minutes, uncovered.

7. Cover the bottom of a 3-quart large casserole dish (with a lid) with half of the bread slices. Ladle enough of the onion and mushroom broth over the bread slices to cover. Add a layer of squash slices and ladle a small amount of broth to cover the squash slices. Repeat with slices of bread, broth, squash slices, and more broth. Combine the cheeses and top the panade with the grated cheese. Place in the oven and cook, covered, for 1 hour. Reduce heat to 350°F, remove the cover, and continue cooking until well browned, 30 minutes longer.

8. To serve, use a spatula to divide the panade among 6 large soup bowls and ladle a small amount of broth over the panade. Serve immediately.

Wine Pairing

The perfect time to try a robust Merlot with plush red fruit.

chicken breasts in calvados sauce with fall panzanella salad in golden balsamic vinaigrette

Calvados, a dry apple brandy from the Normandy region of France, creates a particularly autumnal sauce that works well with both the sweetness of the pear and the slight bitterness of the radicchio. Other country-style sourdough breads, especially ones with ingredients such as nuts and dried fruits, can be used.

SERVES 4

---

panzanella salad

6 slices country-style walnut sourdough bread, cut into ½-inch dice (about 6 cups)

4 tablespoons olive oil

1 shallot (about 1 ounce), minced

2 leeks (about 8 ounces each), white and tender green parts only, split lengthwise, cut into ¼-inch slices, and cleaned and drained thoroughly

2 small pears (about 1 pound), cored and cut into ¼-inch dice

2 cups very thinly sliced radicchio

½ teaspoon salt, or as needed

⅛ teaspoon freshly ground black pepper, or as needed

golden balsamic vinaigrette

3 tablespoons extra-virgin olive oil

2 tablespoons golden balsamic vinegar

¼ teaspoon salt, or as needed

Pinch of freshly ground black pepper, or as needed

chicken breasts in calvados sauce

4 boneless, skin-on chicken breasts (about 2 pounds)

½ teaspoon kosher salt

⅛ teaspoon freshly ground black pepper

¼ cup olive oil

¼ cup Calvados

½ cup dry white wine

1 cup chicken stock

1 tablespoon unsalted butter

---

1. Preheat the oven to 350°F.

2. For the panzanella salad: Toss the bread with 2 tablespoons of the olive oil. Spread evenly on a baking sheet, place in the oven, and toast, tossing frequently, 6 to 7 minutes. The bread cubes should be crisp on the outside and slightly tender and chewy on the inside. Place the bread in a large mixing bowl and reserve until needed.

3. While the bread is toasting, warm the remaining 2 tablespoons of olive oil in a large sauté pan over medium heat. Add the shallot and leeks and sweat, covered, until slightly translucent, about 3 minutes. Add the pears and continue to sweat, covered, for another 2 minutes, stirring occasionally. Add the radicchio and sweat until the radicchio wilts and softens, about 2 minutes. Season the mixture with salt and pepper. Remove from the heat and allow to cool to room temperature. Reserve until needed. Increase the oven temperature to 450°F.

4. For the vinaigrette: Whisk all of the ingredients together and reserve until needed.

5. For the chicken breasts: Pat dry the chicken breasts with a paper towel and season both sides with salt and pepper. Place a wire rack on a baking sheet.

6. In a large, ovenproof sauté pan over medium-high heat, heat the olive oil until it is very hot, but not smoking. Place the chicken breasts, skin-side down, in the pan and cook, undisturbed, until the skin is crispy and golden brown and does not stick to bottom of the pan, about 5 minutes. Using a spatula, turn the chicken breasts over and sauté until golden brown, about 4 minutes longer. Place the chicken breasts on the prepared baking sheet and place in the oven until an instant-read thermometer inserted into the thickest part of the breast registers 165°F, about 10 minutes.

7. If more than a tablespoon or so of oil is left in the sauté pan, drain off the excess. Return the pan to medium-high heat. Mix the Calvados and white wine and pour into the pan, being very careful to avoid the resulting steam and spatter. Deglaze the pan, scraping up any caramelized chicken juices. Bring the liquid to a fast simmer over medium-high heat and reduce the liquid by half, until thickened, 3 to 4 minutes. Add the chicken stock, bring to a fast simmer over medium-high heat, and reduce until saucelike, 4 to 5 minutes. Remove the pan from the heat and stir in the butter.

8. Remove the chicken breasts from the oven and allow to rest for about 5 minutes. Add the pear mixture to the bread cubes and gently mix. Starting with 2 tablespoons of the vinaigrette, toss the panzanella salad lightly to coat, adding more vinaigrette as necessary.

9. To serve, place about ¾ cup of the panzanella salad on each plate. Snuggle a chicken breast against the salad and pool about 1 tablespoon of the sauce next to the chicken. Serve immediately.

Wine Pairing

Try this dish with an off-dry Riesling to match the hints of apple from the Calvados.

Technique:
roasting

As the weather cools, one of the most comforting smells to come from a kitchen is that of meat roasting in the oven. There's something elemental in its appeal, creating a sense of hearth and home and coming inside.

Once you learn the basics, roasting is one of those techniques that can carry you through a lifetime of variations. With the right cut of meat and a few kitchen tools, you'll be able to roast pork, beef, and poultry to crisp and succulent perfection without much fuss.

what is roasting?

Roasting is a cooking method that uses dry heat to deepen flavors and hold in juiciness. Unlike other methods, such as braising, that use slower cooking methods and liquid to tenderize meat and bring out its flavors, when it comes to roasting, the less liquid (which can steam rather than roast) the better. For this reason, be sure that meat is bone-dry before cooking. Once dry, season generously with salt, pepper, and other seasonings and rub into the skin.

searing the meat

There are two ways to sear meat for roasting: One is to sauté at a relatively high temperature, browning the meat before placing it in the oven. Another is to place the meat in the oven at a high temperature and then reduce the oven temperature for the duration of the cooking time. What you're looking for in both methods is the eventual browned meat particles that will form the basis of a sauce.

oven and pan

There are a few crucial components to dry roasting. Bring the meat to room temperature before placing it in the oven, be absolutely sure that your oven temperature is accurate (an oven thermometer is indispensable), and use a pan that is specifically designed for roasting. Ideally, your roasting pan should be heavy, have handles, be no more than 2 to 3 inches deep, and have a rack that fits snugly to promote even browning and keep the meat from coming in contact with fat and juices. The bottom of the roasting pan should be made for stove-top cooking, as

sauces and gravy will be made on top of the stove.

doneness and resting

Although cooking times given in recipes act as a reference point, the best way to determine when a roast is ready is to use an instant-read thermometer or, better yet, one of the new generation of thermometers with probes that stay in the meat while cooking. Meat continues to cook after it is taken out of the oven, and this "carryover" effect can account for up to 10°F—so it is essential to take meat out of the oven before it reaches its desired doneness. Once it's out of the oven, allow the meat to rest for at least 10 minutes. Resting allows juices to relax back into the fibers of the meat, so that they don't all run out when the meat is cut.

deglazing and sauces

Pan juices form the basis of countless sauces. If the meat you are roasting has thrown off a notable amount of fat into the cooking juices, a good place to start is to pour all of the juices into a fat separator. Put the roasting pan on the stove top over medium-high heat. Pour the deglazing liquid (wine, liquor, apple cider vinegar, defatted cooking juices, stock) into the pan and scrape the bottom of the pan while the liquid comes to a boil, incorporating the browned pieces of roasting juices.

Depending upon the sauce, you can then reduce the deglazing liquid, add additional seasonings and stock, and reduce the liquid once again until it reaches a saucelike consistency.

carving and serving

Carving meat at the table has a certain friendliness that keeps the cook engaged with his or her guests. So choose a carving board that's attractive enough to be part of the table and that has wells for the collection of juices. A sharp slicing knife and meat fork make for easy carving and serving.

roasted pork tenderloin with apple and bacon compote

This makes a cozy dinner party for the first golden days and crisp Napa Valley nights of fall. The sweet, tart, and salty compote is prepared while the pork is roasting, so everything is ready at about the same time. Leftovers make inviting sandwiches.

SERVES 8

---

24 fresh sage leaves

Two 1-pound pork tenderloins

1½ teaspoons kosher salt

½ teaspoon freshly ground black pepper

2 tablespoons plus 1 cup canola oil

4 ounces applewood-smoked bacon (about 4 slices), cut into ¼-inch-wide slices

2 garlic cloves, cut into thin slices

1 small white onion (about 8 ounces), peeled, halved, and cut into ¼-inch slices

1 teaspoon fresh thyme leaves

4 tart green apples (about 2 pounds), cored and cut into ½-inch cubes

½ cup unfiltered apple cider

Pumpkin and Sage Polenta (page 131)

---

1. Preheat the oven to 400°F. Mince 8 of the sage leaves and reserve until needed.

2. Bring the tenderloins to room temperature and dry completely with paper towels.

3. Place a roasting rack on a baking sheet. Season the pork with 1 teaspoon of the salt and ¼ teaspoon pepper. In a large sauté pan or skillet over medium-high heat, heat the 2 tablespoons of oil until a sheen develops and the oil begins to separate. Add the pork and brown well and evenly on all sides, turning occasionally, about 2 minutes per side.

4. Remove the pork from the pan (reserve the pan) and place the pork on a roasting rack. Place the pork on the middle rack in the oven and roast until the center of the meat reaches an internal temperature of 145°F for medium-rare (pink in the middle), about 25 minutes, or 150°F for medium, 30 to 35 minutes.

5. While the pork roasts, add the bacon to the reserved pan and cook over medium heat, stirring frequently, until crisp, 6 to 8 minutes. Stir in the garlic and cook for 30 seconds or until aromatic. Stir in the onion, minced sage, and thyme and sauté, stirring and scraping the bottom of the pan for browned bits, until the onion is tender, about 4 minutes. Add the apples and sauté, stirring often, until lightly caramelized and tender, about 5 minutes.

6. Turn the heat to high and add the cider to deglaze the pan. Scrape any remaining browned bits from the bottom of the pan. Lower the heat to medium-high and reduce the liquid to a thick glaze, stirring occasionally, 4 to 5 minutes. Season with the remaining ½ teaspoon of salt and ¼ teaspoon of pepper. Remove from the heat and keep warm.

7. Remove the pork from the oven and cover loosely with aluminum foil. Let stand for 10 minutes. The internal temperature will continue to rise by 5 to 10 degrees.

[recipe continues]

8. While the pork is resting, heat the 1 cup canola oil in a small sauce-pan over medium-high heat. Once the oil is warm enough so that the sage leaves sizzle without smoking, fry the remaining 16 sage leaves until crisp, 10 to 20 seconds. Remove the sage leaves and drain on a plate lined with paper towels.

9. Cut the pork into ½-inch-thick medallions. Arrange the medallions over a bed of pumpkin and sage polenta and border with about ½ cup apple and bacon compote per serving. Place 2 sage leaves on each plate and serve immediately.

Wine Pairing

This recipe can go with reds like a fruity Pinot Noir or with whites such as a rich Riesling or dry Gewürztraminer.

| Chef's Note |

instant-read and probe thermometers

The use of an instant-read or probe thermometer is essential to cooking roasts to the correct doneness. Place the thermometer in the thickest part of the meat, away from any bones. Remember that the meat will continue to cook once removed from the oven, often rising an additional 5° to 10°F in temperature.

Probe thermometers, which are inserted into meat with the digital display resting outside of the oven, are especially useful for larger cuts, when pulling meat in a roasting pan out of the oven is cumbersome.

hanger steak in pinot noir sauce with crispy shallots and point reyes blue cheese

A hanger steak recipe, in one of its many guises, has been on Greystone's restaurant menu since it opened in October 1995. At the time, this cut of beef was relatively hard to find, but today it is more readily available. Properly marinated and grilled, it is one of my favorite beef flavors and has the additional advantage of being an affordable cut of meat.

SERVES 4

---

marinade

1 **cup** olive oil

¼ **cup** red wine vinegar

2 garlic cloves, minced

2 thyme sprigs

Four 8-ounce hanger steaks, trimmed of excess surface fat

crispy shallots

2 **tablespoons** all-purpose flour, for dusting

4 small shallots (about 4 ounces), peeled, cut into ⅛-inch slices and separated into rings

2 **cups** canola oil, for frying

¼ **teaspoon** salt, or as needed

pinot noir sauce

2 **tablespoons** extra-virgin olive oil

2 shallots (about 2 ounces), peeled and finely chopped

1 **cup** Pinot Noir

1 **cup** rich chicken or beef stock

1 **teaspoon** fresh thyme leaves

1 **tablespoon** cold butter

½ **teaspoon** salt, or as needed

⅛ **teaspoon** freshly ground black pepper, or as needed

½ **teaspoon** salt

⅛ **teaspoon** freshly ground black pepper

24 small grapes

4 **ounces** Point Reyes blue cheese (or another blue cheese), at room temperature

---

1. For the marinade: Combine all of the ingredients and mix well. Place the steaks in a nonreactive dish just large enough to hold them. Pour the marinade over the steaks, cover, and marinate in the refrigerator for 3 to 4 hours, turning at least once.

2. For the crispy shallots: While the steaks are marinating, place the flour in a medium bowl. Toss the shallot rings to coat lightly with flour.

3. In a small saucepan over medium-high heat, heat the canola oil (about 2 inches deep) to 360°F. Carefully add the shallot rings and fry until crispy and golden brown, about 1 minute. Remove the crispy shallots with a slotted spoon and drain on a plate lined with paper towels. Sprinkle with the salt and reserve.

4. For the Pinot Noir sauce: In a medium sauté pan over medium heat, heat the olive oil. Add the shallots and sauté until softened but not brown, about 2 minutes.

5. Increase the heat to high, add the wine, and bring to a boil. Reduce the wine to a thick sauce, 4 to 5 minutes. Add the stock and reduce by at least half or until it thickens, about 5 minutes. Add the thyme leaves.

6. Remove the pan from heat and add the butter to finish the sauce. Season with the salt and pepper. Rewarm when ready to use.

7. Light a charcoal fire or turn the grill to medium-high heat.

[recipe continues]

8. Remove the steaks from the marinade and scrape off any marinade still clinging to the meat. Pat the steaks dry with paper towels and season with the ½ teaspoon salt and ⅛ teaspoon pepper.

9. Grill the steaks over a medium-hot for 5 to 7 minutes. Turn the steaks over and grill for another 5 to 7 minutes, or until an instant-read thermometer inserted into the thickest part of the steak registers 125°F for medium-rare.

10. Place the steaks on a cutting board and tent loosely with aluminum foil. Let the meat rest for 10 minutes.

11. While the steaks are resting, warm a small sauté pan over medium-high heat. Add the grapes and roast, shaking the pan, for about a minute. Reserve until needed.

12. Cut the hanger steaks across the grain into ½-inch slices, keeping the slices together. Place the steak on plates and pour the Pinot sauce around the steak. Sprinkle a quarter of the cheese over the top of each steak and a quarter of the crispy shallots over the cheese. Place 6 roasted grapes on each plate and serve immediately.

Wine Pairing

Pull out one of your favorite riper-styled Pinot Noirs for this match.

| Chef's Notes |

wine reductions

When using wine in either sauces or soups, it's important to raise the heat, add the wine, and then reduce by at least half, if not to the point at which most of the liquid has been cooked away, to create a thick, almost syrupy consistency. It's important to reduce the wine before adding stock, as otherwise a touch of the alcohol flavor will remain and you won't get the deep, concentrated flavor that cold-weather dishes ask for.

cutting meat against the grain

With many tougher cuts of beef (such as hanger or flank steak), cutting the meat diagonally against the natural grain of the meat will provide you with a more tender texture.

Lesson in Wine:
champagne uncorked

They're back. The holidays. Parties and all that glitters. Family and fancy food. And, of course, Champagne. But, with so many varieties of Champagne available at your local store, how do you know which one to choose?

Although trying to break sparkling wine down into its many complexities is like trying to count the number of bubbles in a bottle, here are a few things to consider when buying bubbly for celebrations large and small.

To start, *sparkling wine* is the more apt term for wine with bubbles. Technically, only those sparkling wines made in the Champagne region of France can be labeled "Champagne." But most of the better sparkling wines from around the world are made using the *méthode traditionnelle*, a technique that originated in Champagne, and will be marked as such on the label.

There are many designations and types of sparkling wines, from extra-dry to quite sweet, from those using only Chardonnay grapes to those using only Pinot Noir grapes and those that blend several varietals from several years, so,

to simplify a bit, here are three general styles and foods to complement them.

the basic bubbles

Nonvintage (NV) brut is the workhorse and signature blend of any sparkling wine producer. *Nonvintage* refers to the fact that what's in the bottle may be a blend of wine from different years (or vintages). *Brut* means that the wine is dry, with a lack of residual sugars (or sweetness). Master blenders build their reputation on their ability to reproduce the same style from year to year. When you find one you like, you should be able to count on it to taste more or less the same whenever you purchase it. Nonvintage sparkling wines are usually among the least expensive offerings from any producer, ranging from $5 to $40. There is no advantage to aging nonvintage wines, so they should be purchased as fresh as possible and then enjoyed within one year. Nonvintage sparklers are relatively casual wines and pair well with simple foods that are salty, briny, or crunchy, such as Parmesan cheese sticks, oysters, caviar, and even really good potato chips.

true luxury

Tête de cuvée (or "top blend") is the best wine from any single producer. They are made in limited quantities, age well, and are often vintage-designated with a year on the label. Têtes de cuvées can vary from release to release and are the sort of rich, complex, and sophisticated wines meant for memorable moments. Each sparkling-wine house (or producer) designates their tête de cuvée with its own name, such as La Grande Dame (Veuve Clicquot), Cristal (Roederer), Étoile (Domaine Chandon), and DVX (Mumm Napa Valley). These are serious wines with serious price tags, to be savored on their own or with elegant foods, starting with hors d'oeuvres and running through an entire meal with rich foods such as lobster and dishes with cream sauce.

something fun and a bit sweet

Off-dry and sec sparkling wines range from slightly to moderately sweet and are becoming a popular style in

California, where they are perfumed with grapes such as Muscat, Pinot Gris, and Riesling. Still a bit too dry for desserts but lovely with fruits and cheese, these sparklers can be enjoyed on their own and also work well with world cuisines.

Serve the sparkling wine as cold as possible, either iced or refrigerator temperature, but prepare for a pleasant surprise as richer wines will be more flavorful as they warm up, just as with white wines. Keep the bottle cold from beginning to end.

storing and serving

Sparkling wine should be kept in a cool (ideally, 55°F), dark, and slightly humid place, lying on its side. Always open carefully, keeping the bottle at a 45-degree angle and pointed away from people. Remove the top foil, cover the cork with a napkin, loosen the cage, and, holding the cork with a firm grip, turn the bottle to loosen. You should have enough control to remove the cork gently, with the bottle making only a slight hiss. A bottle that's been still for several hours should give you no problem, while one that's been shaken can be troublesome. Pour the wine slowly into the glass so that it doesn't bubble over. Leftovers should be stored with a *bouchon*, a specially designed sparkling wine closure, that maintains the bubbles for about another day.

apple and pumpkin fritters
Warm and crisp, these sweet fritters are best eaten at once, dipped in whipped cream, out of hand.

MAKES ABOUT 2 DOZEN FRITTERS; SERVES 8

1 cup all-purpose flour

2 tablespoons light brown sugar

1 teaspoon baking powder

¼ teaspoon kosher salt

¼ teaspoon ground cinnamon

⅛ teaspoon ground nutmeg

⅛ teaspoon ground cloves

⅓ cup milk

1 large egg, lightly beaten

1 Granny Smith or other firm, tart apple, peeled, cored, and cut into ¼-inch dice

⅓ cup pumpkin purée

1 quart canola or other mild vegetable oil, for frying

2 teaspoons Cinnamon Sugar, for dusting (facing page)

1½ cups Cider-Honey Whipped Cream (facing page)

1. In a small bowl, use a fork to combine the flour, sugar, baking powder, salt, cinnamon, nutmeg, and cloves. Reserve until needed.

2. In a large bowl, combine the milk, egg, apple, and pumpkin and stir well to combine. Sprinkle the flour mixture over the milk mixture and stir gently to just combine.

3. Line a baking sheet with paper towels. In a medium saucepan, heat the canola oil to about 365°F. Gently drop heaping teaspoons of the batter into the hot oil. You'll need to do this in batches so as to not crowd the pan. Fry, turning once, until golden brown and cooked in the middle, about 4 minutes.

4. Use a slotted spoon to transfer the fritters to the baking sheet lined with paper towels. While still hot, sprinkle with the cinnamon sugar. Serve immediately with cider-honey whipped cream.

Wine Pairing
Delightful with a rich Riesling or dry Gewürztraminer as they might drink in Alsace.

cinnamon sugar

MAKES 2 TABLESPOONS

5½ teaspoons sugar

½ teaspoon ground cinnamon, or as needed

Blend the sugar and cinnamon together well and taste. Add more cinnamon as desired.

cider-honey whipped cream

You'll have leftover cider syrup; drizzle it over roasted or grilled pork or poultry, yogurt and fruit, vanilla ice cream, pound cake, oatmeal, or pancakes.

MAKES ABOUT 1½ CUPS

---

cider syrup

2 cups unfiltered apple cider

½ cinnamon stick

In a medium saucepan over medium-high heat, bring the cider and cinnamon stick to a simmer and reduce until the mixture becomes a thick syrup (about ⅓ cup). It will firm up further as it cools. Refrigerate until needed.

---

whipped cream

1 cup heavy cream, chilled

2 tablespoons Cider Syrup, above

2 teaspoons honey

Pinch of freshly grated nutmeg

---

1. Place a large metal bowl and a whisk in the refrigerator to chill for 10 minutes. If using a stand mixer, chill the bowl and whisk attachment.

2. Pour the cream into the chilled bowl. Beat with the chilled whisk until the mixture forms soft peaks. Add the cider syrup, honey, and nutmeg and continue whisking until the mixture forms medium peaks. Cover and refrigerate until needed.

| Chef's Note |

deep-frying at home

When deep-frying at home (yes, you can do it!), a deep-fat frying thermometer and a metal skimmer are essential. Choose a pan large enough to hold the oil with at least 3 inches of space in the pan above the level of the oil. Generally, the oil is heated over a medium to medium-high heat and to 350°F, but that temperature can vary with the food being fried. Cook in small batches (so as to not lower temperature of oil and so that the food does not stick together), skim off particles between batches, and let the oil return to the designated temperature in between batches. If frying a large batch of food, you can keep the cooked food warm in a 200°F oven, but serve as quickly as possible, as fried foods lose their crispness quickly.

And then there's the question of what to do with the leftover oil. If you are frying similar sorts of food within a couple of weeks, strain the completely cooled oil through a piece of cheesecloth or coffee filter into a container that you can seal. Seal the container and keep in the refrigerator. You can probably reuse this oil 3 to 4 times.

persimmon pudding cake

The sight of vibrant orange persimmons hanging from bare-branched trees is one of Napa Valley's most bittersweet and beautiful sights in late fall and a reminder that the harvest here is a year-long affair.

This old-fashioned pudding cake recipe comes from Chef Eve Felder, associate dean for Curriculum Innovation at the CIA's main campus in Hyde Park, New York.

SERVES 8 TO 10

2 tablespoons brandy	**1½ cups** milk
½ cup dried currants	**1 teaspoon** vanilla extract
6 very ripe Hachiya persimmons (1½ to 1¾ pounds), peeled	**1 tablespoon** honey
1¼ cups all-purpose flour	**6 tablespoons** melted butter, slightly cooled
½ teaspoon salt	**¾ cup** sugar
¾ teaspoon baking soda	**1 cup** walnuts, toasted and coarsely chopped
1 teaspoon baking powder	**2 cups** whipped cream (optional)
3 large eggs	

1. Preheat the oven to 350°F

2. Butter a 9-inch springform pan. Place a round of parchment or waxed paper in the bottom of the pan.

3. Pour the brandy over the currants and soak for 30 minutes.

4. Cut the persimmons in half. Cut 3 of the persimmons into ½-inch dice and set aside; this should yield about 1 cup of diced persimmon. Scoop out the pulp from the remaining persimmons with a spoon; this should yield about 1 cup of persimmon pulp. Purée the pulp in a food processor or in a blender until smooth.

5. In a large mixing bowl, combine the flour, salt, baking soda, and baking powder. In another mixing bowl, whisk the eggs slightly; add the persimmon pulp, milk, vanilla, honey, melted butter, sugar, and the currants with the brandy. Add the wet ingredients to the dry ingredients, mixing just until the flour is incorporated. Fold in the chopped walnuts and diced persimmon. Pour the batter into the springform pan and place the pan on a baking sheet.

6. Place in the oven and bake until the cake has pulled away from the side of the pan and the top is firm to the touch, about 1 hour and 45 minutes to 2 hours. Remove the cake from the pan while still warm. Cut into wedges and serve with whipped cream.

Wine Pairing

A little glass of tawny port matches the richness of the pudding and warms you at the end of a chilly day.

| Chef's Note |

ripening hachiya persimmons

There are two main varieties of persimmons in the American marketplace: Hachiyas (astringent) and Fuyu (nonastringent). Hachiya persimmons are picked while still relatively firm and must be completely ripened to be palatable. Ripen inside on a kitchen counter; this process takes about a week. Hachiyas must be almost gooey soft to be ready to use. Ripe persimmon can be puréed and frozen in a plastic bag.

walnut tart with maple ice cream

Michael Pryor, CIA graduate and sommelier of Greystone's restaurant from 1998 to 2006, brings together the East Coast (maple syrup) and the West Coast (new-harvest Napa Valley walnuts) in a dessert that is a much less cloyingly sweet alternative to the classic pecan pie. The success of this recipe depends upon very fresh walnuts, without a lot of tannins. If you can't find some at a farmers' market, there are numerous online sources.

SERVES 8 TO 10

---

1 pound Sweet Tart Dough (page 100)

walnut filling

½ cup cold, unsalted butter, cut into ¾-inch cubes

1½ cups packed light brown sugar

2 large eggs

¾ teaspoon vanilla extract

1 tablespoon black walnut liqueur or bourbon

3 cups shelled walnuts, the freshest you can find

2 cups Maple Ice Cream (facing page)

---

1. Preheat the oven to 350°F.

2. Place the dough on a lightly floured surface and dust a small amount of flour over the dough. Roll out the dough to approximately 11 inches in diameter. If the dough begins to stick, dust the work surface with a little more flour. Invert the dough onto a 10-inch tart pan, press the dough into the corners, and trim off any excess that rises above the pan walls. Place in the freezer for 30 minutes before baking.

3. Line the tart shell with parchment paper and fill with dried beans or pie weights. Bake until the edges are light brown, about 20 minutes. Turn the heat down to 325°F, remove the parchment and the weights, and bake until lightly golden and cooked through, an additional 10 minutes. Cool completely before filling.

4. Increase the oven temperature to 375°F.

5. For the walnut filling: Using a mixer fitted with the paddle attachment, cream the butter with the brown sugar on medium speed until smooth and light in color, 2 to 3 minutes. Add the eggs one at a time. Add the vanilla extract and liqueur and mix until blended. Remove the bowl from the mixer and gently fold in the walnuts.

6. Spread the filling evenly over the partially baked tart crust and bake until the filling browns slightly, 18 to 20 minutes. Cool before cutting and serve with maple ice cream.

maple ice cream

A few quick notes on making ice cream: The base must be very cold before it is added to the ice cream maker. The best way to accomplish this is to refrigerate it overnight. Also, to get full flavor and the smoothest texture, allow the frozen ice cream to temper, or soften, a bit in the refrigerator before serving.

MAKES ABOUT 1 QUART

1¾ **cups** whole milk

¾ **cup** heavy cream

1 **cup** Grade B maple syrup (do not use Grade A as the flavor is too delicate)

5 large egg yolks, room temperature

Pinch of salt

1. In a heavy-bottomed saucepan over low heat, heat the milk and cream until hot but not boiling.

2. While the milk mixture is heating, combine the maple syrup, egg yolks, and salt in a mixing bowl. Whisk until thick and opaque, about 2 minutes.

3. Slowly whisk about a third of the milk mixture into the egg yolk mixture, then combine with the rest of the milk mixture in the saucepan, whisking constantly. Slowly heat and stir constantly until the mixture coats the back of a wooden spoon, about 6 minutes.

4. Immediately strain through a fine sieve and refrigerate until chilled completely, preferably overnight. Freeze in an ice cream maker according to the manufacturer's instructions. For best flavor, temper the ice cream for 15 minutes before serving.

Wine Pairing

Though they're not easy to find, there are a few sweet sherries from California that are amazing with this nut tart. The hunt is worthwhile.

dormancy

Winter in wine country is the briefest of seasons, a quiet interlude of softened sun and deepened shadow. Crowds recede, and long-welcome rains coax the ground to a brilliant green again. Bare grapevines etch the vineyards in repose. Mother-of-pearl clouds—alabaster, salmon, and gray—sink into indigo hills at sunset, which now comes on quickly. It is a time of slumber and solitude, of pruning, of the land lying fallow.

On the forested hillsides, Douglas firs whisper and chanterelles await discovery under the moist leaves of valley oak trees. Velvety moss pillows rocks in now-coursing creek beds, and filigreed lichen drapes gracefully from branches. In the nearby ocean, sweet Dungeness crab and briny oysters are brought up from cold West Coast waters.

Whether you are cooking in wine country or somewhere else, winter is a time to come in, slow down, gather 'round. A fire is made, dinner started, a bottle of red wine opened to exhale. The cycle of the growing season is hushed, not so much finished, as readying its roots for the year to come.

Soups such as Greystone Gruyère Onion Soup (page 171) and White Bean Soup with Chanterelles and Sage (page 170) bring a welcome, hearthlike warmth to dark, stormy days, while jewel tones of pomegranate seeds and citrus in Wine Country Winter Salad (page 167) and Dungeness Crab Salad with Grapefruit and Avocado (page 168) brighten both the table and the mood.

The winter-night appeal of melted cheese in soulful foods can be found in Wild Mushroom Lasagna with Ricotta and Bellwether Farms Crescenza Cheese and Spinach (page 182) and Spinach, Caramelized Shallots, and Gruyère Soufflé (page 180). Caramelized juices and slow-simmering, house-filling smells of red wine and garlic can be had in Cabernet-Braised Short Ribs with Swiss Chard and Orecchiette (page 195) and San Francisco's seafood-inspired and bay leaf–scented Cioppino (page 184).

lemongrass crab and scallop cakes with cucumber dipping sauce

Light and delicate, these fragrant cakes allow the fresh flavors of the crab and scallops to come through. Note that the seafood needs to marinate overnight.

This recipe comes from Holly Peterson, who has been teaching Food and Wine Dynamics at Greystone since the college opened its doors in 1995.

SERVES 6

---

scallop and crab cakes

12 ounces sea scallops (about 8 scallops)

12 ounces fresh lump crabmeat (about 1 Dungeness crab, cooked and cleaned)

3 stalks fresh lemongrass

4 large eggs

¼ cup finely chopped fresh chives

Zest of 2 lemons, julienned (Meyer lemons, if available)

½ cup fine fresh bread crumbs

½ teaspoon salt, or as needed

¼ teaspoon freshly ground black pepper

dipping sauce

1 cup water

¼ cup sugar

1 teaspoon sea salt

¼ cup white vinegar

Pinch of red pepper flakes, or as needed

1 large shallot (about 2 ounces), peeled and finely minced

½ English cucumber, peeled, cut in half lengthwise, seeded, and cut into ⅛-inch slices

¼ cup peanut oil

¼ cup butter

6 cilantro sprigs, for garnish

6 mint sprigs, for garnish

---

1. For the crab cakes: Remove the tough muscle on the side of the scallops and cut the scallops into ¼-inch dice. Combine the scallops and crabmeat in a large bowl. Remove the outer skin from lemongrass, cut each stalk into a couple of pieces, and crush the pieces to release flavor. Place the lemongrass in the bowl with the scallops and crab, cover the bowl, and marinate overnight in the refrigerator.

2. Remove the lemongrass pieces and discard. Add the eggs, chives, lemon zest, and bread crumbs to the fish. Gently mix to incorporate the ingredients. Season the mixture with the salt and pepper. Reserve in the refrigerator until ready to cook.

3. For the dipping sauce: Bring the water to a boil and add the sugar and sea salt, stirring to dissolve. Remove from heat and add the vinegar, red pepper flakes, shallot, and cucumber. Stir to mix the ingredients and refrigerate until ready to use.

4. Form the scallop and crab mixture into 18 cakes that are about 2 inches in diameter.

5. Heat a large sauté pan over medium-high heat and add the peanut oil and butter. As soon as butter melts, add the cakes and sauté until just lightly golden and warmed through, about 1 minute on each side. Be careful not to overcook, and cook in batches if necessary to avoid crowding the pan. Serve 3 cakes per plate along with a small ramekin of cucumber dipping sauce. Garnish each plate with a cilantro and mint sprig.

Wine Pairing

A nonmalolactic Chardonnay with some lemony notes and crisp acids would work well with this dish.

wine country winter salad

wine country winter salad The crisp bite of pomegranate seeds and the pear, the sweetness of the fruit and balsamic vinaigrette, and the bright jewel-like color make this salad a refreshing contrast to rustic, long-braised winter dishes. Don't cut the fruit until ready to serve. The balsamic vinaigrette makes about ¾ cup and a 1-pound pomegranate will yield about ¾ cup of seeds.

SERVES 6

balsamic vinaigrette

1 shallot (about 1 ounce), minced

2 tablespoons balsamic vinegar

2 teaspoons sherry vinegar

Pinch of salt

6 tablespoons canola oil

2 tablespoons walnut oil

salad

2 heads Belgian endive, trimmed and separated into leaves

1 small head of frisée, cored and separated into leaves

2 cups loosely packed arugula, carefully washed and dried

½ cup pomengranate seeds (see Chef's Note)

2 Asian pears (6 to 8 ounces each), peeled, cored, and thinly sliced

2 ripe Fuyu persimmons (6 to 8 ounces each), peeled and cut into thin wedges

1. For the vinaigrette: Combine the minced shallot, vinegars, and salt and let sit for 30 minutes. Whisk in the oils.

2. Toss the greens, pomegranate seeds, Asian pears, and persimmons with ¼ cup of the vinaigrette to lightly coat, adding more vinaigrette as necessary.

Wine Pairing

Dry Muscat is a keen choice to complement the fruits in this salad.

| Chef's Note |

pomegranate seeds

Pomegranate seeds add a crunchy and juicy accent to many a fall and winter salad. To seed a pomegranate, have a large bowl of cold water at hand. Cut the crown off of the pomegranate, place it in water, and break the pomegranate apart along several membranes. Using your hands, hull the seeds from the skin and membrane. Drain the water and pull out the pomegranate skins and membrane, leaving behind the seeds. Seeds will keep, covered in the refrigerator, for about a week.

dungeness crab salad with grapefruit and avocado

I knew I was somewhere else entirely when during my first winter in Napa Valley, I found myself picking grapefruits, lemons, and oranges from the trees in my backyard. Their tropical brilliance and intoxicating fragrance lend winter in wine country an exotic allure that brightens even stormy days.

Citrusy, briny, and silky, this salad is a reflection of a simple dish made with ingredients at the peak of their seasonal flavor. It is a colorful and refreshing way to start a heavier winter meal, or it can be a light lunch accompanied by some great bread. You can substitute lobster, cooked rock shrimp, or other crabmeats.

SERVES 4

lemon vinaigrette

2 tablespoons fresh lemon juice

¼ teaspoon sugar

¼ teaspoon kosher salt, or as needed

Pinch of freshly ground black pepper

½ teaspoon grated lemon zest

¼ cup extra-virgin olive oil

salad

8 ounces fresh lump Dungeness crabmeat

2 teaspoons grated lemon zest

2 tablespoons mayonnaise

2 tablespoons crème fraîche

2 tablespoons minced fresh chives

2 cups loosely packed curly cress, watercress, or micro-greens (about 4 ounces)

2 small Red Ruby grapefruits (about 12 ounces each), peeled and cut into segments

2 small avocados (6 to 8 ounces each)

Sea salt, as needed

Freshly ground black pepper, as needed

1. For the vinaigrette: Whisk all of the ingredients except the olive oil together in a medium mixing bowl. Whisk in the olive oil to emulsify. Reserve until needed.

2. For the salad: Place the crabmeat, lemon zest, mayonnaise, crème fraîche, and chives in a medium mixing bowl. Using two forks, gently toss the ingredients together until just combined. Reserve in the refrigerator until needed.

3. Starting with 2 tablespoons of the vinaigrette, lightly toss the greens with the vinaigrette and add more dressing as needed, 1 tablespoon at a time, to lightly coat. Reserve in the refrigerator until needed.

4. Just before serving, fan out the segments from half a grapefruit (4 or 5) on to each of 4 salad plates. Cut the avocados in half, remove the pits, and peel back the skins. Cut each half into ½-inch slices. Alternate the slices from half an avocado with the grapefruit segments on each salad plate. Drizzle about 2 teaspoons of vinaigrette over each plate of grapefruit and avocado.

5. Divide the dressed greens among the 4 plates (about ½ cup per plate). Mound a quarter of the crab mixture in the center of the greens. Sprinkle each serving with sea salt and freshly ground black pepper.

Wine Pairing

Try to find a lean, lemony Sauvignon Blanc to pair with the winter citrus in this salad.

citrus

To get those close-to-perfect citrus segments without the pith, the first rule is to use very sharp knives. With a chef's knife, cut off the top and bottom of the citrus, enough so that the top of each segment shows through without white pith. Stand the citrus on one of the flat ends. Carefully carve off the peel, following the curved contour of the fruit. Then, using a sharp paring knife, cut parallel to and just inside the membranes that separate the segments. Don't try to cut alongside the membrane or your chances of the segment breaking apart increases.

microplanes

Using a grating Microplane creates the delicate, almost fluffy zest that works so well in dressings and salads. Just be sure to not grate deeply into the white (and bitter) pith.

white bean soup with chanterelles and sage

If you can find chanterelles, this is the dish to use them in. Their earthy flavor and golden oak color finishes the hearty bean and musky sage flavors. If not available, you can use other wild or deeply flavored mushrooms such as porcini or shiitake.

SERVES 6

6 thyme sprigs

6 parsley sprigs

2 bay leaves

10 black peppercorns

¼ **cup** olive oil

1 small white onion (6 to 8 ounces), cut into ¼-inch dice

2 leeks (about 8 ounces each), white and tender green parts only, split lengthwise, cut into ¼-inch slices, and cleaned and drained thoroughly

1 small fennel bulb (about 1 pound), trimmed, cored, and cut into ¼-inch dice

2 celery stalks (about 3 ounces), cut into ¼-inch dice

2 garlic cloves, peeled and thinly sliced

Two 15-ounce cans organic great Northern white beans, or 1 cup dried great Northern or other small white beans, soaked in water for at least 8 hours and simmered until soft

6 **cups** light chicken or vegetable stock

3 **tablespoons** butter

8 **ounces** chanterelles or other mushrooms, thinly sliced

2 **tablespoons** very thinly sliced fresh sage leaves

2¼ **teaspoons** kosher salt, or as needed

½ **teaspoon** freshly ground white pepper, or as needed

6 **tablespoons** dry white wine

2 **tablespoons** heavy cream (optional)

3 **teaspoons** white truffle olive oil or extra-virgin olive oil, for drizzling

1. Tie the thyme, parsley, bay leaves, and peppercorns into a cheesecloth sachet. Reserve until needed.

2. In a large heavy-bottomed soup pot over medium heat, warm the olive oil. Add the onion, half of the leeks, the fennel, celery, garlic, and the sachet. Sweat the ingredients, stirring frequently, until the vegetables are well softened and the onion is translucent, 8 to 10 minutes.

3. Add the beans and stock, bring to a boil over medium-high heat, reduce to a simmer, and cook uncovered until the soup has thickened a bit, about 35 minutes.

4. While the soup is simmering, melt the butter in a medium sauté pan over medium heat. Add the chanterelles, the remaining leek, and the sage. Sauté the mixture until the mushrooms are soft, 4 to 5 minutes. Season with ¼ teaspoon of the salt and a couple of grinds of white pepper. Increase the heat to medium-high, add the wine, and cook, stirring frequently, until the liquid is almost evaporated. Remove the pan from the heat and reserve.

5. Remove the sachet from the soup. Purée half of the soup (about 3 cups) and return to the pot. Stir well to blend and season with the remaining 2 teaspoons of salt and the remaining pepper. Add the reserved mushroom mixture.

6. Bring the soup to a gentle simmer over medium to medium-high heat and simmer, uncovered, until the soup has thickened a bit more, about 15 minutes. If adding cream, add during the last 5 minutes of simmering.

7. Ladle a generous cup of soup into warmed bowls. Drizzle each bowl of soup with ½ teaspoon white truffle oil. Serve immediately.

Wine Pairing

Dolcetto, with its full, earthy flavors but light, fresh texture, is a winner with this warming soup.

greystone gruyère onion soup

Part soup, this signature dish from Greystone's restaurant is topped with a dramatic white cloud, yet it's a mostly make-ahead dinner party offering: Everything except whipping the egg whites can be done in advance; in fact, the soup is best when made ahead.

SERVES 6

---

soup

2 tablespoons olive oil

3 large yellow onions (about 10 ounces each), cut into thin slices

½ teaspoon freshly ground black pepper

2 teaspoons kosher salt, or as needed

¼ cup white wine

2 quarts good-quality brown chicken stock

1 bay leaf

2 teaspoons fresh thyme leaves

1 tablespoon sugar

1 tablespoon plus 1 teaspoon fresh lemon juice, or as needed

6 thin slices soft white bread

soufflé

¼ cup unsalted butter

¼ cup all-purpose flour

1½ cups whole or part-skim milk

1½ cups grated Gruyère cheese, plus **6** thick slices

Pinch of cayenne pepper

1 teaspoon fresh lemon juice

2 tablespoons white wine

½ teaspoon kosher salt

6 large egg whites, at room temperature

¼ cup grated Parmesan cheese

---

1. Preheat the oven to 350°F.

2. For the soup: In a medium stock or soup pot over medium-low heat, warm the olive oil. Add the onions, pepper, and 2 teaspoons salt and decrease the heat to low. Cook, stirring occasionally, until the onions are well caramelized (a deep, golden brown), 30 to 40 minutes.

3. Raise the heat to high and deglaze pan with the wine, scraping up any browned bits of caramelized onion from the bottom of the pan. Simmer for 1 minute.

4. Add the chicken stock, bay leaf, and thyme. Bring to a boil and reduce the heat to a simmer. Simmer for 20 minutes. Stir in the sugar and lemon juice. Proceed with cooking or cool and refrigerate the soup up to 24 hours.

5. While the soup simmers or when it is rewarming, trim the bread to fit inside of ovenproof soup bowls that are about 5 inches in diameter. Place the trimmed bread slices on a baking sheet and toast in the oven until golden, about 10 minutes. Remove from the oven and set aside. If making ahead, cool and reserve in a zip-close bag at room temperature.

6. For the soufflé: In a large saucepan over medium-low heat, melt the butter. Add the flour and whisk constantly until the roux is well blended and begins to bubble. Add half of the milk, whisking constantly, until the milk is completely blended and there are no lumps. Repeat with the remaining milk. Raise the heat to medium so that the mixture is gently bubbling. Be careful not to scorch the bottom of the pot.

[recipe continues]

7. Continue to whisk until the sauce is smooth, shiny, and thickened, about 4 minutes. Add the grated Gruyère cheese and stir until it completely melts into the sauce. Stir in the cayenne, lemon juice, wine, and salt. Remove from the heat but keep warm. If using later, cool, cover with plastic wrap, pressing the wrap onto the surface, and refrigerate.

8. About 15 minutes before you want to serve the soup, bring it to a simmer over medium heat. Readjust the seasoning with lemon juice and salt, if needed. Remove from the heat. If necessary, gently rewarm the soufflé batter over a double boiler.

9. In the bowl of an electric mixer fitted with the whip attachment or in a large bowl with a handheld electric mixer, beat the egg whites on medium-high speed until medium-stiff peaks form. With a rubber spatula, gently fold one-third of the egg whites into the soufflé base. Repeat with the remaining egg whites and then stir in the Parmesan cheese, gently folding the mixture until completely combined.

10. Fill the soup bowls three-quarters full of soup. Top with a round of the toasted bread and then a slice of Gruyère. Using a rubber spatula, gently spoon one-sixth of the soufflé batter onto the bread. Carefully place the soup bowls on a baking sheet and transfer to the oven. Bake until the soufflé is well risen and golden brown, about 20 minutes. Serve immediately.

Wine Pairing

A great opportunity to bring out a lush Chardonnay—one that's got oaky richness and butteriness and even a couple of years of age.

simply cooked beans with new-pressed olive oil

Napa Valley breeds a certain sort of food rebel, the kind who won't accept food that's just a commodity. Even the humble bean has found its advocate in Steve Sando of Rancho Gordo, who grows heirloom varieties of beans throughout Northern California. Try to find new-harvest olive oil if possible, as its young, fruity essence is the perfect "finishing" flavor.

From Michael Chiarello, TV host, cookbook author, chef-owner of Bottega Restaurant in Yountville, California, and founder of Napa Style.

SERVES 6

---

1 cup dried white heirloom beans, such as Cellini or Zolfini

6 tablespoons extra-virgin olive oil

½ onion (about 4 ounces), peeled and cut into ¼-inch dice

1 carrot (about 2 ounces), peeled and cut into ¼-inch dice

2 celery stalks (about 3 ounces), trimmed and cut into ¼-inch dice

1 bay leaf

1 quart water, or as needed

2 teaspoons sea salt, or as needed

½ **teaspoon** freshly ground black pepper

---

1. Soak the beans overnight in enough water to cover them by a couple of inches.

2. Drain the beans. In a large pot or stockpot over medium heat, warm 2 tablespoons of the olive oil. Add the onion, carrot, and celery and sauté until the vegetables are softened, 4 to 5 minutes. Add the beans, bay leaf, and enough water to cover by about 2 inches.

3. Bring the water to a boil over medium-high heat. Reduce the heat to a simmer and cook, skimming off any foam that rises to the surface, until the beans are softened but not mushy, about an hour. Watch the level of the water and maintain it at 2 inches above the beans so that they don't go dry.

4. Add the salt and pepper, stir, and let the beans cool slightly in their cooking liquid. Remove the bay leaf. There should be enough water left to create just a bit of "sauce." Pour off any excess water. Pour in the remaining ¼ cup of the olive oil, stir, and adjust the seasonings.

oven-roasted brussels sprouts with fennel seeds

In lieu of having a wood-fired oven (in which Michael Chiarello cooks the Brussels sprouts and which is incomparable), roasting the Brussels sprouts in a very hot oven creates a char that makes the sprouts surprisingly sweet.

SERVES 6

---

1 teaspoon fennel seeds

2 pounds Brussels sprouts, stemmed and cut in half

1 teaspoon sea salt

½ teaspoon freshly ground black pepper

¼ cup extra-virgin olive oil

---

1. Preheat the oven to 500°F.

2. In a small skillet over medium-low heat, toast the fennel seeds until fragrant, shaking the pan almost constantly, about 2 minutes. Immediately pour the seeds onto a plate. Cool and then grind in a clean coffee or spice grinder to a powderlike consistency. Reserve until needed.

3. Remove any tough outer leaves from the Brussels sprouts. Bring a large pot of well-salted water to a boil over high heat. Have a large bowl with ice water on hand. Add the Brussels sprouts to the boiling water and blanch for 1 minute. Drain and immediately place in the ice water until completely chilled. Drain again, then place on a baking dish or large platter lined with paper towels. Allow the Brussels sprouts to dry completely, then refrigerate if not using right away.

4. In a large mixing bowl, toss the Brussels sprouts with the salt, pepper, fennel seeds, and olive oil. Transfer them to a baking sheet or large ovenproof skillet. Place in the hot oven and roast, shaking the pan occasionally, until the Brussels sprouts are tender and lightly charred, about 10 minutes. Serve immediately.

Lesson in Wine:
cabernet sauvignon

As the foundation for many of the greatest wines in the world, the Cabernet Sauvignon grape not only captures the imagination of both winemakers and wine drinkers around the globe, but also holds that interest throughout a lifetime.

Why are wines made from the Cabernet Sauvignon grape so special? The grape's rich fruit flavors offer depth and a certain lyricism to the structure of the tannins that are so prominent in the grape. This structure makes possible the often elegant aging of many of the best Cabernets. The influence of oak in the aging process and the artistry of blending Cabernet with other grapes come together to create the complexity for which this varietal is justifiably famous.

Just a few decades ago, benchmark Cabernet Sauvignon would have come from Bordeaux, France, where it's grown and used prominently, along with what is known as its "Bordeaux family" of grapes—Merlot, Cabernet Franc, Malbec, and Petite Verdot—in some of the most sought-after wines in the marketplace. Now the talent and pride of Napa Valley grape

growers and winemakers, in tandem with the region's unique soils and microclimates, have made *Napa Valley Cabernet Sauvignon* among the first words in the language of the varietal.

There may be no season like winter to settle in and enjoy this soul-satisfying red. A natural complement to rich flavors, slow-cooked dishes, and long, chilly nights—preferably in front of a fire—"Cabs," like many a lifelong friendship, reveal themselves over time.

---

a few general styles

Cabernet Sauvignon has many consistent qualities regardless of where it's produced. Red fruits, black currant (or crème de cassis), bell pepper, olives, mint, and eucalyptus are among them. As the wine ages, the oak character from the barrel changes from spiced to forest floor, tobacco, and fermented tea aromas. Wines made from this grape are often quite tannic (bitter, astringent) in their youth, giving the sensation of rough sandpaper or soft fuzzy carpet on the tongue, depending on how well the tannins are managed in the winemaking process. Though tannins are one of the very things that help Cabernet

Sauvignon age well, expect them to be noticeably softer in an older wine.

While it's difficult to break it down simply, one could try to classify three different styles of wine made from Cabernet Sauvignon in the California wine country.

Wines you might be able to find and afford easily for everyday drinking are made from a high percentage of Cabernet Sauvignon—even 100 percent. They have a gentle oak influence and are from places like Sonoma County, Mendocino, and Lodi. These wines should provide the essence of the grape, with fresh, fruity flavors—red currants, green olives, and warm baking spices—in a nicely balanced wine that would most likely be best within just a couple years of the vintage.

Blended Cabs are another popular style practiced by a good number of California producers. By adding Merlot, Cabernet Franc, Petite Verdot, Malbec, or other grapes like Syrah, Zinfandel, or Sangiovese, the winemaker's aim is to provide layers of flavors and a thoughtful structure by maximizing the best qualities of all their fruit. By law, to label a wine Cabernet Sauvignon in California, it must contain at least 75 percent of that grape; the rest can be a mix of whatever grape or grapes the winemaker desires. Flavors vary depending on the grapes used, but look for the same Cab essence throughout, enhanced by the different aromas and flavors—berries, plums, florals, and spices—or structural elements—tannins, acids, color—that the other varietals bring to the blend.

The final style category—from a single wine made by a small producer or one offering of many from larger wineries—is quite well known by wine enthusiasts and goes by many names: cult wine, limited production, single vineyard, estate, reserve, super-luxury, ultra-premium. Take your pick; they all can translate into high-end, high-priced, highly sought-after and desirable wines. The best of these wines are ones of exquisite balance and can be either 100 percent Cabernet Sauvignon or blended with other varietals. In the flavor and nose, expect to find voluptuous red, blue, and black fruits and nearly transcendental surprises, among them Indian spices, meaty savoriness, sweet pastry notes, black tea, good coffee, forest floor, and pipe tobacco.

a brief riff on foods that love cabernet sauvignon

With young Cabs, pair rich foods. It's well known and documented that fat will cut tannin and vice versa. Grilled steaks (the bitterness from the grilling helps with the bitterness of the tannins), rich fatty cheeses, and hearty braises all work well. With older wines, keep the food simple and the bold flavors to a minimum: Roasted meats or earthy foods allow the wine to shine. We often think of just red meat dishes, but in fact eggplant, tomatoes, olives, bitter greens, and even the right fish preparation can all work deliciously with Cabernet Sauvignon.

serving, storage, aging

Serve at slightly below room temperature, 55° to 65°F, or at least make sure the bottle is cool to the touch. Many wines can age well in a cool, dark place if left undisturbed for a few years. The best wines from the best vintages can age for several decades even, developing an intriguing bottle character, and become soft in the mouth, with a complex, mature bouquet and a rich yet delicate expression. Many solid, good-value wines can also become more than fresh and fruity if carefully aged for a short time, even just a year. Older wines may need to be decanted from the bottle slowly, using a candle to see when pouring should stop to leave sediment behind, and a very young bottle may benefit from a powerful decanting, which makes the wine splash vigorously, to accelerate the aeration of the wine, making it more approachable and less hard on the palate. Use a generously sized glass for maximum enjoyment.

spinach, caramelized shallots, and gruyère soufflé

Out of humble ingredients an ethereal meal is created. With a simple green salad, chunks of hearty bread, and a bottle of wine, you'll have a winter meal meant for hearth and home.

SERVES 6

---

4 tablespoons cold unsalted butter

½ cup grated Parmesan cheese

4 large eggs, separated, plus **2** large egg whites

10 ounces baby spinach

2 teaspoons kosher salt

1 cup milk

2 shallots (about 4 ounces), peeled and cut into ⅛-inch slices

3 tablespoons all-purpose flour

¾ cup grated Gruyère cheese (about 3 ounces)

Pinch of grated nutmeg

½ teaspoon freshly grated black pepper

2 tablespoons finely minced fresh chives

⅛ teaspoon cream of tartar

---

1. Butter a 1½-quart soufflé dish with 1 tablespoon of the butter. Sprinkle the Parmesan cheese over the bottom and sides, shaking to coat the surfaces. Reserve in the refrigerator until needed.

2. Place the 4 egg yolks in a medium bowl and beat lightly with a fork.

3. Place the spinach in a 6-quart soup pot or stockpot over medium-high heat. Sprinkle with ½ teaspoon of salt, stir, sprinkle with another ½ teaspoon of salt, stir, and cover. Cook for 2 minutes, uncover, stir, and cook until the spinach has just wilted but is still a deep green, about another 2 minutes. Drain the spinach in a colander and rinse with cold water to stop the cooking. Squeeze the excess moisture from the spinach and chop into 1-inch pieces. This can be done in advance and refrigerated. Bring to room temperature before using in the soufflé.

4. In a small saucepan, warm the milk to about 98°F.

5. In a medium saucepan over medium-low heat, melt the remaining 3 tablespoons of butter. Add the shallots and sauté, stirring frequently, until they have softened and are beginning to caramelize, about 10 minutes. Add the flour and cook, stirring constantly and scraping the bottom of the pan, until the butter and flour mixture is just bubbly but without letting it brown, 3 to 4 minutes. Slowly whisk in the warmed milk, along with the Gruyère cheese. Bring the mixture to a simmer and cook, stirring continuously, until the sauce has thickened, about 4 minutes. Place the base in a large stainless-steel bowl. Beat a small amount of this warm mixture slowly into the egg yolks and then add the egg yolk mixture back into the warm base. Stir in the nutmeg, remaining 1 teaspoon salt, pepper, chives, and the spinach. Keep the base warm, but not hot. If refrigerating, place in a double boiler or other sort of water bath to rewarm before using in the soufflé.

6. Preheat the oven to 425°F.

7. In a stainless-steel bowl, using a stand or hand mixer, beat the 6 egg whites with the cream of tartar until the whites will hold a medium peak, 3 to 4 minutes.

8. Gently and quickly fold the whites into the base a third at a time. Pour into the prepared soufflé dish and place in the middle of the oven. Cook for 15 minutes, reduce the heat to 375°F, and cook until the soufflé is puffed and golden brown, an additional 15 to 20 minutes (cook for the longer time if you want a firmer soufflé).

9. Remove the soufflé from the oven. With two large spoons back to back, open the center of the soufflé and spoon out one-sixth of soufflé onto each plate. Serve immediately.

Wine Pairing

A barrel-fermented Sauvignon Blanc with some oak is a light way to echo the round flavors of the cheese.

a few pointers on making soufflés

beating egg whites

The trick to getting egg whites to whip up beautifully is to not have any fat in the whites or on the bowl or beaters used to beat the egg whites. Carefully separate the egg yolks from the whites (not a smidgeon of yolks in the whites!), and rinse the stainless-steel bowl and beaters with a touch of vinegar before using. It's better to underbeat rather than overbeat egg whites, so watch carefully.

tempering

When mixing ingredients of different temperatures and consistency, it's best to introduce a bit of the colder ingredient(s) to the warmer ingredient(s) to gradually meld the two temperatures. In the case of soufflés, this will be done when introducing the egg yolks to the warm base and again when introducing the egg whites to the base.

wild mushroom lasagna with ricotta and bellwether farms crescenza cheese and spinach

This lasagna is a rich once-a-winter creation, meant for a fire and a favorite bottle of Cabernet Sauvignon. It is elevated to regal by the handcrafted crescenza cheese from Bellwether Farms in Sonoma County. Teleme cheese is a fine substitute. Sautéing the spinach and mushrooms can be done in advance. In fact, I think the entire lasagna is best made a day in advance and reheated.

SERVES 6 TO 8

---

1 pound fresh lasagna pasta

½ cup olive oil

¼ cup minced shallots

2 teaspoons fresh thyme leaves

1½ pounds mushrooms (wild mushrooms such as chanterelles or, if not available, a combination of cremini and portobello), cut into ¼-inch slices

¾ teaspoon kosher salt, or as needed

¼ teaspoon freshly ground black pepper, or as needed

1 pound baby spinach

velouté

1 quart chicken stock

¼ cup unsalted butter

¼ cup all-purpose flour

½ teaspoon kosher salt

Freshly ground white pepper

15 ounces whole-milk ricotta cheese (about 2 cups)

7 ounces crescenza cheese

1 cup freshly grated Parmigiano-Reggiano cheese

---

1. Preheat the oven to 375°F.

2. Cut the pasta into enough pieces to make three layers in a 9-by-13-by-2-inch glass lasagna pan. You may have extra pasta, as these sheets come in different sizes.

3. In a large stockpot over high heat, bring 8 quarts of salted water to a boil. Have three 13-inch pieces of waxed or parchment paper on the counter. Add the pasta sheets to the water and cook according to the package directions until al dente, about 3 minutes. Drain carefully so as not to rip the sheets. Spread the drained pasta out on the waxed paper and brush the pasta with about 1 tablespoon of olive oil. Press a second piece of waxed paper on top of the pasta sheets. Turn the sheets over, carefully pull back the waxed paper, and brush the other side of the pasta with another tablespoon of olive oil. Press the sheets of waxed paper back onto the pasta. Stored this way, the pasta will keep at room temperature for a couple of hours.

4. In a large soup pot, heat ¼ cup of the olive oil over medium heat. Add the shallots and thyme and sauté until lightly golden, about 4 minutes. Add the mushrooms, toss to coat with the oil and shallots, and sauté until the mushrooms are golden, just tender, and have released their liquid, about 10 minutes. Turn the heat to medium-high and cook until most of the liquid has evaporated, about 4 minutes. Season with ½ teaspoon of the salt and ⅛ teaspoon of the black pepper. Reserve until needed (this will make about 3 cups). This can be made up to a day in advance and refrigerated.

5. In a large stock or soup pot, heat the remaining 2 tablespoons of olive oil over medium-high heat. Add the spinach, toss to coat with the oil, and sauté until wilted, about 5 minutes. Season the mixture with the remaining ¼ teaspoon of salt and ⅛ teaspoon of black pepper. Reserve until needed (this will make about 2 cups). This can also be made up to a day in advance and refrigerated.

6. To make the velouté: In a 3-quart saucepan over medium-high heat, bring the chicken stock to a simmer.

7. In a heavy 3-quart saucepan, melt the butter over low heat. Add the flour to the butter and cook, stirring continuously, until the roux is very lightly browned and fragrant, about 4 minutes. Gradually add the stock, whisking constantly, until the stock and roux are well blended. Bring the mixture to a simmer over medium to medium-low heat and simmer, stirring frequently to incorporate any skin that forms, until the velouté is thick enough to coat the back of a spoon, about 30 minutes. Season with the salt and a few grinds of white pepper.

8. Pour one-third of the velouté (about 1 cup) into the bottom of the lasagna dish. Gently lay enough pasta sheets to cover the velouté evenly. Evenly sprinkle half of the spinach (about 1 cup), mushrooms (about 1½ cups), and ricotta (about 1 cup) over the pasta, making sure to bring the ingredients evenly to the edges. Drizzle ½ cup velouté over the layers. Gently place another layer of pasta sheets over the ricotta. Repeat with the remaining spinach, mushrooms, ricotta, and ½ cup velouté. Gently place another layer of pasta sheets on top. Spread the remaining velouté over the last layer of pasta. Break the crescenza into tiny pieces (this cheese is gooey, so do your best to squeeze it into ½-inch pieces) and sprinkle evenly over the surface. Sprinkle the Parmesan evenly over the dish.

9. Cover the lasagna with a piece of aluminum foil and place on the middle rack of the oven.

10. Bake for 30 minutes. Uncover and rotate the dish in the oven. Bake the lasagna until bubbly and golden, 20 to 25 minutes. Remove from the oven and let sit for at least 15 minutes before serving.

Wine Pairing

Look for a full-bodied, ripe, oaky Napa Valley Cabernet Sauvignon to stand up to the robust flavors in this hearty dish.

cioppino

Cioppino is a San Francisco tradition, originally from the city's Italian North Beach neighborhood. It makes good use of the abundance of fresh seafood that Northern California is blessed with, the star of the show being Dungeness crab. But this seafood stew can be tailored to wherever you're digging into a midwinter meal; with the exception of the crab and clams, it can be made, in a pinch, with frozen seafood. We serve it for a Christmas Eve wine country celebration, made easier in that you can (and perhaps should) prepare the base a day in advance. This is a communal meal, with crackers and picks in hand, extra bowls for shells, and no fancy napkins!

SERVES 6, GENEROUSLY

¾ **cup** olive oil, or as needed, plus extra for drizzling

4 **teaspoons** minced garlic

2 leeks (about 8 ounces each), white and tender green parts only, split lengthwise, cut into ¼-inch slices, and cleaned and drained thoroughly

1 **tablespoon** fresh thyme leaves

2 **teaspoons** chopped fresh oregano

½ **teaspoon** red pepper flakes

2 **teaspoons** kosher salt, or as needed

½ **teaspoon** freshly ground black pepper, or as needed

1 small fennel bulb (about 12 ounces), trimmed, cored, and cut into ¼-inch dice

1 green bell pepper (about 8 ounces), cored, seeded, and cut into ¼-inch dice

1 celery stalk (about 2 ounces), sliced thinly

1 carrot (about 2 ounces), peeled and cut into ¼-inch dice

2 **tablespoons** tomato paste

3 **cups** dry white wine

1 bay leaf

One 28-ounce can of diced tomatoes, with juices

2 **cups** fish stock

1 **tablespoon** Worcestershire sauce

1 sourdough baguette, cut into twelve ½-inch slices

1 garlic clove, cut in half

18 manila or cherrystone clams (about 1 pound), well scrubbed

1 **pound** firm-fleshed white fish, such as halibut or sea bass (or a combination of the two)

8 **ounces** large shrimp (21/30 count), peeled and deveined

8 **ounces** scallops (if large, cut into ½-inch pieces)

1 Dungeness crab (2 to 2½ pounds), cooked, cleaned, and cracked into 2- to 3-inch pieces, claws broken into 2 pieces and body cleaned of meat

¼ **cup** chopped fresh flat-leaf parsley

2 **tablespoons** chopped fresh basil

---

1. In a heavy-bottomed soup pot over medium heat, warm ½ cup of the olive oil. Add the garlic and leeks and sauté until the leeks are softened, about 4 minutes. Add the thyme, oregano, red pepper flakes, salt, pepper, and fennel and continue sautéing until the fennel has begun to soften, about 4 minutes. Add the green pepper, celery, and carrot and sauté until the last batch of vegetables has softened, about 4 minutes.

2. Add the tomato paste and stir into the vegetable mixture until the tomato paste begins to caramelize a bit, about 1 minute. Turn the heat to high and add 2 cups of the white wine. Scrape any caramelized bits on the bottom of the pot and reduce heat to medium-high. Simmer and reduce the white wine by half, about 5 minutes. Add the bay leaf, tomatoes and their juices, fish stock, and Worcestershire sauce and bring the cioppino base to a gentle simmer over medium heat. Cover and cook until the cioppino base has thickened slightly, about 30 minutes. Remove the bay leaf and coarsely purée the base, until the vegetables are completely pulverized but there is still some texture to the purée (not completely smooth). Adjust the seasonings with the salt and pepper. The cioppino base can be made a day ahead up to this point and refrigerated.

3. Preheat the broiler.

4. Use the remaining ¼ cup olive oil as needed to brush the sourdough baguette slices and then rub with the cut sides of the garlic cloves. Discard the cloves. Toast lightly under the broiler. Remove from the oven and place in the soup bowls. Keep warm.

5. In a large skillet with a cover over medium heat, warm the remaining cup of white wine. Add the clams, cover, and steam, shaking the pan occasionally, until most of the clams open, about 5 minutes. Discard any unopened clams. Remove the rest of clams from the pan and keep warm.

6. Strain the remaining liquid through a piece of cheesecloth in a colander and add to the cioppino base.

7. Add the white fish, shrimp, and scallops to the base, stir to combine, and simmer over medium heat until the shrimp has begun to turn pink, about 4 minutes. Add the clams and crab pieces and simmer for 3 more minutes. Add the parsley and basil, stir to combine, and simmer 2 more minutes.

8. Ladle the cioppino into the warmed soup bowls over the toasted sourdough, trying to get a selection of seafood in each serving. Serve immediately.

Wine Pairing

Vibrant Italian varietal rosés, with their fuller flavors but high acidity, would stand up to the chorus of flavors in this soulful dish.

| Chef's Note |

Don't use commercial clam juice. Although it's getting harder to find the bones from white-fleshed fish needed to make a fish stock or fumet, there are lots of good frozen fish stocks around. You can also save shrimp shells, freeze them, and from time to time make a simple stock from them.

gently baked salmon with zinfandel, shallots, edamame, and celery root purée

Here's an example of a well-paired "red wine with fish" dish, as the spices in the rub act as a bridge to the many spicy tones often associated with Zinfandel. The recipe is another from Food and Wine Dynamics instructor Holly Peterson, who finds the slow baking of the salmon in low heat a particularly moist way to cook this fish. There will be enough spice mixture to make this recipe twice.

SERVES 6

---

spice mixture

½ **teaspoon** black peppercorns

½ **teaspoon** cumin seeds

½ **teaspoon** coriander seeds

1½ **teaspoons** dry mustard

1½ **teaspoons** sugar

1½ **teaspoons** sea salt

shallot mixture

1 **tablespoon** unsalted butter

½ **teaspoon** sugar

½ **teaspoon** light grey sea salt (see Chef's Note)

8 small or 4 large shallots (about 8 ounces total), peeled and cut into ⅛-inch slices

1 **cup** Zinfandel

edamame

1 **cup** fresh or frozen shelled edamame

½ **teaspoon** light grey sea salt

Freshly ground black pepper

¼ **cup** chicken stock

1 **teaspoon** high-quality extra-virgin olive oil

1 **teaspoon** minced fresh marjoram or oregano

celery root purée

2 celery roots (about 2 to 2½ pounds each), without leaves

1½ **cups** milk (whole, 2 percent, or soy milk) or cream, or as needed, depending on desired thickness

½ **cup** chicken stock

1 **tablespoon** butter, softened, or as needed

2 **tablespoons** heavy cream (optional)

½ **teaspoon** salt

⅛ **teaspoon** ground white pepper

Pinch of ground nutmeg

6 salmon fillets, all skin and bones removed, 5 to 6 ounces each

---

1. For the spice mixture: In a clean coffee or spice grinder, grind the spices finely, about 4 seconds. Reserve until needed.

2. For the shallot mixture: In a 10-inch sauté pan over medium-low heat, melt the butter. Add the sugar and salt and stir to blend. Add the shallots and sauté until the shallots are well coated with the mixture, about 2 minutes. Add the wine, stir to blend, and cook until all of the wine has evaporated and the shallots are well caramelized, 45 to 50 minutes, stirring the mixture occasionally as the wine takes on a jamlike consistency. Keep the mixture warm until needed.

3. For the edamame: If the edamame are frozen, blanch according to package directions. Drain.

4. In a 1½-quart saucepan over medium heat, warm the edamame, salt, pepper, and chicken stock until just heated through, about 2 minutes. Just before serving, drizzle the olive oil onto the edamame and stir in the marjoram until blended. Keep warm until needed.

5. For the celery root purée: Peel and cut the celery roots into ½-inch cubes just before using to keep them from turning brown. Place the celery root cubes in a large skillet with enough milk to almost cover. Bring to a simmer over medium-high heat, reduce the heat to medium, and cook, covered, until the celery root is tender, 20 to 25 minutes.

6. In a blender, purée the celery root, milk, and chicken stock until smooth. Return to the pan. Add the butter and stir gently to melt and incorporate. Add more milk or cream as desired to reach a smooth consistency. Season the mixture with salt, pepper, and nutmeg. Keep warm until needed.

7. Preheat the oven to 250°F.

8. Place the salmon fillets on a baking sheet. Rub ½ teaspoon of spice mixture onto each salmon fillet. Place on the middle rack in the oven and bake until *tremblant* (barely translucent in the center and a little wiggly to the touch), about 20 minutes. Cover to keep warm, if necessary.

9. Place a cup or so of the celery root purée on each plate. Nestle a salmon fillet up against the purée and sprinkle the shallots over the salmon. Spoon 2 heaping tablespoons of edamame onto each plate. Serve immediately.

Wine Pairing

Really light, fruity Zinfandel is a surprise hit with this complex fish entrée.

| Chef's Note |

light grey sea salt

Hand harvested in small batches on the coast of France, light grey sea salt has a clean, ocean taste that brings a complex, minerally flavor to food. Fleur de sel can usually be substituted.

braising

In winter, with more time spent nestling in to slow-simmering dishes and dark red wines, braised meals afford a relaxed meandering through an afternoon of savory aromas that warm and calm stormy days.

what is braising?

Braising is a method of slow, moist cooking that creates intensely flavored, fork-tender morsels from tougher cuts of meat that are often less expensive than tender cuts. Meals can be started early in the day and left in the oven, where the flavors of humble ingredients meld into something greater than the sum of their parts. Many braised dishes are best cooked a day in advance, making them a good choice for entertaining, and provide welcome leftovers throughout the week.

In essence, most braises combine browned meats, aromatics such as bay leaves, onions, and herbs, and a cooking liquid or two. The liquid actually steams the meat, inducing the ingredients to release their flavors, become tender, and create nuanced sauces. Braising requires very little from the cook and can often be both an economical and relatively easy way to serve classic bistro and trattoria fare that is a buffer to winter's chill.

what to have on hand

For braising, the heavier the cookware for even heat distribution and retention, the better. The pot should be deep enough to hold a large piece of meat but not as tall as a stockpot. A favorite piece of equipment for braising is an enameled cast-iron Dutch oven. There are also low-sided pots called *braisiers* made especially for braising. Look for tight-fitting lids and choose pieces that keep ingredients snug while simmering, without too much space next to or on top of ingredients. If you want to have to use only one pot, cookware should be able to be used on both the stove top and in the oven.

Unbleached parchment paper is another part of the braising repertoire. By placing a piece of parchment paper over the pot before putting the lid on, you'll be trapping the steam along with the braising liquid that bathes the meat.

step by step

The first step in preparing most slow-cooking braised dishes is to brown the outside of the meat, as browning caramelizes the meat and helps create depth of flavor in the finished dish. Meat should be close to room temperature, blotted dry with paper towels, and seasoned with salt and pepper just before cooking. Heat the oil in the pot over medium-high heat so that the meat sizzles when it is laid into the oil, and then deeply brown (don't char) all sides of the meat. Use just enough oil to coat the bottom of the pan and pour off the excess fat after browning and before adding vegetables or liquid to the pot. If you are braising meat in pieces, you'll often need to do this in batches so as not to crowd, and thus steam, the meat while trying to create a crispy crust. The meat is then removed from the pot while the vegetables sauté and the pot is deglazed.

For cold-weather braises, red wine is often the cooking liquid of choice, but stock as well as other liquids are also used. Wine is usually added after the meat has been browned and the vegetables cooked, by increasing the heat to at least medium-high and adding the wine to deglaze the pan. Scrape the bottom of the pan with a wooden spoon to include any browned bits in the sauce. Typically, the wine is reduced by about half.

Once the meat is back in the pot, additional braising liquids can be added, but only to bring liquids about a third of the way up the side of the meat, which produces the proper conditions for steam to tenderize the meat, condense flavors, and create a concentrated sauce.

Bring the liquids to almost boiling (technically, this is 180°F) and reduce to a gentle simmer. To create a low and constant heat, most braises are then put into a preheated oven. This is where the slow factor comes into play, as braises are cooked at relatively low oven temperatures over a long period of time. This "slow and long" approach allows for the meat's connective tissue to soften, melt, and thicken the liquid into a sauce.

Once the meat is lusciously tender, remove the pot from the stove. I like to make the braise in advance to this stage, refrigerate it overnight, skim off the congealed fat and rewarm. You can also tilt the pan to one side and, using a large spoon, skim off the layer of fat that has risen to the surface. If the sauce is not thick enough, remove the meat and place the pot over medium heat, reducing to the desired consistency.

braised chicken thighs with red pearl onions, green olives, golden raisins, roasted garlic gremolata, and orzo

The inspiration for this dish came from an abundance of lemons in the citrus groves that welcome visitors to Greystone. The sweet and salty combination of the olives and raisins is brought to life with the addition of the fragrant citrus and herb gremolata.

The sauce that is created is rich enough to coat all of the ingredients without any butter being added.

Thank you to chef-instructor Almir DaFonseca.

SERVES 4

chicken

One 10-ounce package red pearl onions

8 bone-in, skinless chicken thighs (about 2½ pounds)

½ cup all-purpose flour, for dredging

1 teaspoon salt

½ teaspoon freshly ground black pepper

2 tablespoons olive oil

1 cup white wine

1 cup rich chicken stock

½ cup pitted picholine olives (or other small green olives), cut in half lengthwise

½ cup golden raisins

gremolata

6 tablespoons finely grated lemon zest

6 tablespoons minced fresh flat-leaf parsley

5 garlic cloves, peeled and finely minced

3 to 4 teaspoons olive oil, or enough to just moisten and bind gremolata

orzo

1 cup orzo

1 tablespoon olive oil, or as needed

½ teaspoon salt

¼ teaspoon freshly ground black pepper

---

1. For the chicken: Preheat the oven to 325°F.

2. Bring at least 2 quarts of water to a boil. Add the pearl onions and blanch just until the skins have loosened, about 1 minute. Drain. When cool enough to handle, cut off the root tip and pop the onions from their skins. Reserve in the refrigerator until needed.

3. Rinse the chicken thighs under cold water and pat dry. Mix together the flour, salt, and pepper and place in a shallow dish. Lightly dredge the chicken thighs in the flour mixture, shaking off any excess.

4. Warm the olive oil in a large skillet over medium-high heat for 1 minute. Add four of the chicken thighs, bone-side up, in the pan. Sear the thighs until a golden crust forms, about 4 minutes. Turn and sear until a golden crust forms on the second side, 3 to 4 minutes. Place the seared thighs on a plate. Repeat with the remaining chicken thighs.

[recipe continues]

5. Discard the oil in the pan and increase the heat to medium-high. Deglaze the pan with the wine, scraping up any browned bits on the bottom of the pan. Reduce the wine by half, about 4 minutes. Add the chicken stock and bring to a boil over high heat. Add the reserved pearl onions, the olives, and raisins and bring back to a boil. Decrease the heat to medium (the liquid should be at a simmer) and add the chicken thighs. Bring the liquid back to a simmer, place a piece of parchment paper on top of the skillet, cover, and place the pan in the oven. Cook until the meat is falling away from the bone, 45 to 50 minutes.

6. While the chicken is cooking, make the gremolata. Place the lemon zest and parsley in a small bowl. Warm a 6-inch skillet over medium-low heat. Add the garlic and, stirring constantly, dry-roast the garlic until you see some of the garlic's oil released on the bottom of pan and the garlic has just a touch of golden color, 2 to 3 minutes. Do not allow the garlic to brown. Immediately spoon the garlic into the zest and parsley. Stir well to combine. Starting with 3 teaspoons of olive oil, combine the oil with the garlic mixture to bind the ingredients together. The mixture should be moist but not wet. Add another teaspoon of olive oil, if needed. Reserve at room temperature until needed.

7. For the orzo: In a 3-quart saucepan, bring at least 8 cups of water to a boil over high heat. Add the orzo, bring back to a boil, reduce the heat to medium-high so that water is at a high simmer, and cook for 8 minutes, stirring once in a while to keep the orzo from sticking to the bottom of pan. Remove the pan from the heat and allow the orzo to sit for 5 minutes. Drain well. Place in a bowl and add the olive oil, salt, and pepper. Mix well. Add more olive oil, if needed, to moisten the orzo and mix well. Keep warm until ready to serve.

8. Remove the chicken from the oven. Remove the thighs from the pot and place on a plate. Cover loosely with aluminum foil to keep warm. Place the pot over medium-high heat and reduce the liquid to a loose saucelike consistency, about 4 minutes.

9. Place the orzo on a serving platter or divide equally among 4 individual serving plates. Place the chicken thighs on top of the orzo and spoon the sauce with the onions, olives, and raisins over the chicken thighs and orzo. Spoon about 1 teaspoon of gremolata over each chicken thigh and serve immediately.

Wine Pairing

A fuller-bodied Pinot Gris would pick up both the sweet and savory notes in this dish.

| Chef's Note |

Other uses for gremolata: Combine with equal parts low-fat mayonnaise for a fish or tunafish sandwich, serve over simply prepared white fish, or mix it with more olive oil for a lemony vinaigrette and serve over arugula.

grilled beef tenderloin with plum and soy Lettie and Ted

Hall of Longmeadow Ranch are at the forefront of keeping grazing land open in Napa Valley. The lush green hillside grasses of winter provide the fodder (quite literally!) for Longmeadow Ranch's grass-fed Highland beef. If using grass-fed beef, cook at a somewhat lower temperature and a bit less time, as the meat's naturally lean make-up requires less heat.

This Asian take on a steakhouse recipe is from Master Chef Adam Busby, CIA Greystone's director of education and a dedicated grill master. In creating the marinade, Chef Busby wanted to bridge flavors to those of deep red wines such as Zinfandel, including plum and soy sauce. Another consideration was balancing sweet (apple juice), sour (balsamic vinegar), salty (soy sauce), and bitter (the char of the fire on the meat), while the light touch of fat in the meat acts to mitigate the tannins in many red wines.

SERVES 6

---

marinade

½ **cup** olive oil

¼ **cup** balsamic vinegar

4 garlic cloves, peeled

2 shallots (about 2 ounces), peeled

2 **cups** prune juice

1 **cup** apple juice

½ **cup** soy sauce

1 **tablespoon** fresh rosemary leaves

1 **tablespoon** fresh thyme leaves

1 **teaspoon** freshly ground black pepper

Six 8-ounce filet mignons

---

1. For the marinade: Place the ingredients in a blender and blend on high speed until all of the ingredients are finely puréed, 20 to 30 seconds.

2. Pound the steaks to about 1 inch thick with a meat mallet. Place the steaks in a nonreactive casserole dish large enough to hold the steaks and marinade. Pour the marinade over the steaks, cover, and refrigerate overnight. If the marinade does not completely cover the steaks, turn once.

3. One hour before cooking, drain the steaks and pat dry to get rid of excess marinade. Bring the steaks to room temperature. Light a charcoal fire or turn a gas grill to medium-high.

4. Cook the steaks for about 6 minutes on each side, or to about 125°F on an instant-read thermometer. You may need to move them on and off direct heat if they are scorching.

5. Remove the steaks from the grill, cover loosely with aluminum foil, and allow to rest for 5 minutes before serving.

Wine Pairing

The hard-to-beat classic Cabernet Sauvignon and steak combination plays itself throughout the entire meal.

cabernet-braised short ribs with swiss chard and orecchiette

When you want to sink deeply into a cold winter night, with the murmur of friends around a table, try this deep-into-the-mood-of-dormancy dish. The caramelized flavors of meat juice and tomato paste combine with the concentrated red wine flavors, with a hint of orange peel far in the background.

This is a great way to entertain, as most of the preparation can be done in advance, filling your home with a welcoming aroma of slowly simmered, savory ingredients. It is also a relatively inexpensive meal to serve a crowd, as a little meat goes a long way. The short ribs with their sauce are served with the Swiss chard and pasta in one large bowl, keeping things "pass-around" simple.

Wine Country Winter Salad (page 167) makes a crisp and brilliant accompaniment.

SERVES 6 TO 8

---

short ribs

6 meaty short ribs (about 4 pounds)

1 teaspoon salt

½ teaspoon freshly ground black pepper

2 tablespoons olive oil

1½ cups chopped onions

1 carrot, peeled and cut into ¼-inch dice

1 celery stalk (about 4 ounces), trimmed and cut into ¼-inch dice

2 plump garlic cloves, peeled and minced

2 tablespoons tomato paste

One 750 ml bottle Cabernet Sauvignon

1 bay leaf

6 fresh parsley stems

4 fresh thyme sprigs

2 pieces orange zest, each about 2 inches long by ½ inch wide

1 to 2 cups low-sodium chicken stock

orecchiette and chard

1 pound dried orecchiette

3 tablespoons olive oil

2 plump garlic cloves, peeled and minced

1 cup finely chopped onion

2 bunches Swiss chard (about 1 pound each), ribs removed, cut into ¼-inch slices, well rinsed, and drained (about 12 loosely packed cups)

½ cup freshly grated Parmigiano-Reggiano cheese, plus more for topping

---

1. For the short ribs: Preheat the oven to 325°F.

2. Trim the thick layers of external fat from the short ribs. Don't overdo it; small amounts of fat will create flavor and most of the fat will be removed when the recipe is degreased toward the end. Season all sides of the short ribs with the salt and pepper.

3. In a heavy pot such as a 5-quart stockpot or Dutch oven that has a tight-fitting lid, warm the oil over medium-high heat. Add 3 of the short ribs and sear on all sides until brown, 4 to 5 minutes per side. If there is a lot of exposed meat on the ends, use tongs to stand the ribs up to sear the ends for about 2 minutes per end. Remove the short ribs from the pot and place on a plate or shallow dish. Repeat with the remaining short ribs (you may need less time to brown sides, as the oil will be really hot by now). Reserve until needed.

[recipe continues]

4. Pour off all but 2 tablespoons of the fat from the pan. Reduce the heat to medium and add the onion, carrot, and celery to the pan, scraping up any browned pieces of meat from the bottom of the pan with a wooden spoon. Sauté, stirring often, until the vegetables are lightly browned, about 8 minutes. Add the garlic and, stirring constantly, sauté until just fragrant, about 1 minute longer. Add the tomato paste and, stirring continuously, sauté until the tomato paste just begins to caramelize, 1 to 2 minutes longer.

5. Raise the heat to high and deglaze the pan with the wine, scraping up any browned juices from the bottom of the pot with a wooden spoon. Reduce the heat to medium-high and reduce the wine by half at a high simmer, 12 to 15 minutes.

6. Add the bay leaf, parsley, thyme, and orange zest. Add the short ribs back to the pot. Add enough chicken stock to bring the liquid halfway up the ribs. Bring the stock to a boil, place a piece of parchment paper on top of the pot, cover tightly, and place in the oven. Cook for 2 to 2½ hours, or until the meat is falling off the bone.

7. Remove the short ribs from the pot and place on a platter. When cool enough to handle, shred the meat from the bones into bite-size pieces, discarding any visible fat or gristle. Keep warm until needed.

8. Strain the Cabernet sauce through a fine-mesh sieve, pressing the back of a large spoon on the solids to extract the maximum amount of sauce. Degrease the sauce either by using a gravy separator, tilting the pan to one side and skimming the fat off with a large spoon, or making the dish up to this point the day before, refrigerating it, and spooning off the layer of fat that congeals on the surface. Place the degreased sauce in a large skillet over medium-high heat and reduce to a light sauce consistency (thick enough to coat the back of a spoon), 4 to 5 minutes if the sauce is warm. Keep the sauce warm on low heat.

9. For the orecchiette and chard: Bring a large pot of salted water to a boil. Add the orecchiette and cook according to package directions until al dente, about 12 minutes.

10. Meanwhile, in a large soup pot or stockpot, warm the olive oil for 1 minute over medium heat. Add the garlic and onion and sauté, stirring frequently, until very lightly colored, 6 to 8 minutes. Add the chard, toss well to coat with the olive oil, and sauté, stirring frequently, until softened, about 6 minutes. This will seem like a lot of chard when you first put it in the pot, but it will wilt down considerably. Ladle a cup of the pasta cooking water over the chard and continue to sauté, stirring frequently, until most of the liquid is evaporated, about 4 minutes.

11. Drain the pasta and add to the chard mixture. Pour half of the Cabernet sauce over the pasta and chard and toss to coat the pasta with the sauce. Add the cheese to the pasta and stir well to combine. Place the pasta on a serving platter or divide among large pasta bowls. Place the shredded meat in the remaining Cabernet sauce and warm through over medium heat. Spoon the meat and sauce over the pasta. Serve immediately with additional grated Parmigiano-Reggiano cheese.

Wine Pairing

A great Cabernet Sauvignon is naturally called for when you braise with the same varietal. You can trade up from the braising wine if you like.

brandied dried fruit french tartlets with pecan streusel

These elegant, individual tarts, reminiscent of the flavors of fruit cake, are perfect with a sip of port during the holidays. They have become a holiday gift-giving tradition, as it is simple to make the recipe in steps, and they hold well for a couple of days. The square molds are much easier to use than individual fluted tart molds.

From the Baking and Pastry Arts Certificate Program at Greystone.

MAKES 2 DOZEN TARTLETS

---

fruit compote filling

1 Granny Smith apple (8 ounces), peeled, cored, and cut into ¼-inch dice

2 ounces dried figs, cut into ¼-inch dice

2 tablespoons dried cranberries

¼ cup dried currants

4 large dried apricots (about 4 ounces), cut into ¼-inch dice

½ vanilla bean, split and scraped

1 cup water

⅓ cup sugar

2 teaspoons brandy

Pinch of ground cloves

¼ teaspoon ground cinnamon

Juice of 1 lemon

pecan streusel

⅓ cup finely chopped pecans

½ cup all-purpose flour

2 tablespoons sugar

¼ teaspoon ground cinnamon

Pinch of salt

¼ cup cold butter, cut into small cubes

2 pounds 1-2-3 Tart Dough, shaped into 2 squares and chilled (page 199)

½ cup confectioners' sugar, or as needed

---

1. For the fruit compote: Add all of the ingredients to a medium saucepan and stir to combine. Bring the mixture to a simmer over medium heat and cook, stirring occasionally, until the fruit is tender, 8 to 10 minutes. Cool the mixture on rimmed baking sheets. The liquid will thicken as the compote cools.

2. For the pecan streusel: In a medium mixing bowl or the bowl of a stand mixer, toss together the pecans, flour, sugar, cinnamon, and salt.

3. With a pastry cutter or with the paddle attachment, cut the butter into the flour mixture until the mixture just comes together and has a crumbly texture. Store the streusel in the refrigerator until ready to use.

4. Preheat the oven to 350°F.

5. Let one piece of the dough soften until it indents easily from gentle finger pressure. Roll the pastry into a rectangle about ⅛ inch thick. Cut twelve squares of dough half an inch larger than the rim of the 2½-inch tartlet molds. Lay the dough squares inside the molds, pressing into the corners and sides. Trim off any excess that rises above the mold walls with a sharp paring knife. Dock or prick each tartlet with a fork. Refrigerate the tart shells until ready to fill. Repeat the process with the other piece of dough. The scraps from first piece can be incorporated into the second piece of dough. You should have 24 tartlet shells.

[recipe continues]

6. Line up the molds on two baking sheets. Place 1 tablespoon of filling into each shell. Sprinkle 1 teaspoon of the streusel over the filling.

7. Place the tarts in the oven. Bake until golden brown, about 15 minutes.

8. Remove from the oven and cool on wire racks. While cooling, lightly dust with confectioners' sugar. When cool enough to handle, insert a sharp-tipped knife between the dough and the inside of each tart pan and carefully pop the tartlet out.

Wine Pairing

An elegant California tawny port will highlight both the dried fruit and nuts in these little gems.

1-2-3 tart dough

1-2-3 refers to the approximate proportions of the ingredients: 1 part sugar, 2 parts butter, 3 parts flour (by weight). Cake flour is used, as it is low in gluten and thus does not shrink. You can use this recipe wherever a "short" dough recipe is indicated.

MAKES 2 POUNDS DOUGH (ENOUGH FOR 24 TARTLETS OR TWO 10- OR 11-INCH TARTS)

¾ **cup** sugar

1 **cup** butter, softened

½ **teaspoon** vanilla extract

2 egg yolks, at room temperature

3½ **cups** cake flour

1. In a stand mixer fitted with the paddle attachment, cream together the sugar, butter, and vanilla on medium speed just until smooth and light, 2 to 3 minutes. Add the egg yolks one at a time, scraping the bowl and paddle as necessary between additions.

2. Slowly add the flour, with the mixer running, just until the mixture comes together as a thick, ragged dough. Divide the dough in half, shape into disks or squares, wrap in plastic, and refrigerate for at least 30 minutes.

flourless chocolate cake with dried cherry–cabernet reduction sauce

The combination of the dried cherry Cabernet sauce with this flourless chocolate cake from Greystone's Baking and Pastry Certificate Program is a very grown-up way to end a meal (hopefully with some last sips of the meal's Cabernet Sauvignon!). Please note that both the cake and the sauce need to be started a day in advance.

MAKES ONE 8-INCH CAKE; SERVES 10 TO 12

---

1 tablespoon plus 1 cup unsalted butter

8 large eggs, at room temperature

1 pound bittersweet chocolate

Confectioners' sugar, for dusting

1 cup Dried Cherry–Cabernet Reduction Sauce (facing page)

---

1. Preheat the oven to 325°F.

2. Grease the sides of an 8-inch cake pan with the 1 tablespoon butter and line the bottom with a parchment paper circle. You can buy these circles precut or place the bottom of the pan on a sheet of parchment paper and trace and cut a circle.

3. In a stand mixer or using a hand mixer, start whipping the eggs at low speed and gradually raise the speed to medium-high over about 20 seconds. Whip the eggs until they double in volume, about 5 minutes.

4. Melt the chocolate and the 1 cup butter over a water bath (see Chef's Note). Bring the water to a simmer over medium heat and place the bowl in the pot. Melt the chocolate and butter, stirring frequently, about 4 minutes. You want the mixture to be warm but not hot. It should be a little warmer than body temperature, registering 110°F on an instant-read thermometer.

5. Gently fold one-third of the eggs into the chocolate mixture until only a few streaks of egg are visible. Fold in the remaining eggs until the mixture is all one color and texture, about 3 minutes. At first the mixture may seem runny, but after a few minutes of blending it will thicken. Pour the mixture into the prepared cake pan and smooth the surface.

6. Place the cake pan in another pan with sides that are higher than at least halfway up the cake pan. An ideal combination is placing the 8-inch cake pan inside a 9-inch square pan. Pour boiling water into the outer pan so that it comes halfway up the sides of the cake pan.

7. Place the pans on the middle rack of the oven. Bake until the cake has risen slightly, the edges are just beginning to set (at this stage the cake will have a firm pudding sort of feel to it), and the center registers 140°F on an instant-read thermometer, 20 to 25 minutes.

8. Cool the cake on a wire rack in the pan and refrigerate overnight.

9. To remove the cake from the pan, carefully immerse the pan in a shallow basin of hot water. Shake the pan slightly to make sure there is movement before flipping cake onto a flat cake plate. Dust with confectioners' sugar just before serving.

10. Cut the cake into 12 pieces. Place a slice of cake on a serving plate and pour about 4 teaspoons of the sauce alongside the cake.

Wine Pairing

Look for any of California's great Cabernet Sauvignon–based ports to make this a truly memorable dessert experience.

table of equivalents

The exact equivalents in the following tables have been rounded for convenience.

liquid/dry measurements

U.S.	Metric
¼ teaspoon	1.25 milliliters
½ teaspoon	2.5 milliliters
1 teaspoon	5 milliliters
1 tablespoon (3 teaspoons)	15 milliliters
1 fluid ounce (2 tablespoons)	30 milliliters
¼ cup	60 milliliters
⅓ cup	80 milliliters
½ cup	120 milliliters
1 cup	240 milliliters
1 pint (2 cups)	480 milliliters
1 quart (4 cups, 32 ounces)	960 milliliters
1 gallon (4 quarts)	3.84 liters
1 ounce (by weight)	28 grams
1 pound	448 grams
2.2 pounds	1 kilogram

oven temperature

Fahrenheit	Celsius	Gas
250	120	½
275	140	1
300	150	2
325	160	3
350	180	4
375	190	5
400	200	6
425	220	7
450	230	8
475	240	9
500	260	10

lengths

U.S.	Metric
⅛ inch	3 millimeters
¼ inch	6 millimeters
½ inch	12 millimeters
1 inch	2.5 centimeters